The End of Tolerance?

THE END OF
TOLERANCE?

Alfred Herrhausen Society
for International Dialogue

NICHOLAS BREALEY
PUBLISHING

London

First published by Nicholas Brealey Publishing in association
with Intercultural Press in 2002

Nicholas Brealey Publishing
3–5 Spafield Street
London EC1R 4QB
England
Tel: (+44) 207 239 0360
Fax: (+44) 207 239 0370
www.nbrealey-books.com

Intercultural Press
P.O. Box 700
Yarmouth, Maine 04096
U.S.A.
Tel: (+1) 207 846 5168
Fax: (+1) 207 846 5181
www.interculturalpress.com

Alfred Herrhausen Society for International Dialogue
Tel: (+49 69) 91 03 43 57
Fax: (+49 69) 91 03 60 90
www.alfred-herrhausen-society.org

A Deutsche Bank Forum

The works of art reproduced in this book are part of the
Deutsche Bank Collection.

Editors:
Susan Stern
Elisabeth Seligmann

Translation team led by Igor Reichlin:
Jim Kerr
Derek Whitfield
The Koenen family
Jesús Gutiérrez Vidal

Coordination:
Maike Tippmann

The Alfred Herrhausen Society thanks Dorothee v. Tippelskirch
and Berrit Barlet

ISBN 1-85788-317-9
British Library Cataloguing in Publication Data
A catalogue record for this book is available from the British Library

Printed in Germany

TABLE OF CONTENTS

THE PILLARS OF TOLERANCE: FAITH AND RELIGION

EPILOGUE

APPENDIX

PROLOGUE

ROLF-E. BREUER

FREEDOM'S TWIN

Whether we see it as an opportunity or as a threat – we all live in a global village and we cannot help but rub shoulders with each other: Africans, Americans, Asians or Europeans, Hindus, Jews, Muslims, Christians or Buddhists – in short, people with the widest range of cultural, religious, political or economic traditions and attitudes.

And those suburbs of the global village that are a step ahead in their development have to deal with a further factor: the growing inner complexity of societies, the diversity of lifestyles and values.

An active understanding of tolerance is increasingly becoming imperative in the attempt to ensure that the global village does not deteriorate into a place of terror. Conflicts are inevitable in a world that is growing ever closer together. What counts above all else now is our approach to solving these conflicts and our learning how to integrate the unknown – concepts and peoples – into our world, and vice-versa.

Deutsche Bank had good reason to choose the motto "With an Open Mind – Tolerance and Diversity" as its theme for the year 2002. As we worked with last year's theme "education", we became increasingly aware that true learning – if it is to be more than just training – ultimately focuses on tolerance, on the acceptance that no single individual holds the key to the ultimate truth. And that we need to search for ways to ensure that a peaceful balance can be struck between differing standpoints without any of them necessarily having to be relinquished. Respect for the individual and for the way he chooses to live his life must form the core of the political, philosophical and economic liberalism which our societies so eagerly claim as their foundation.

Deutsche Bank is a citizen of the global village – and can be found in nearly all of its "suburbs". Our company reflects the diversity of the global village – both in our employees and in our customers. At present, more than 98,000 employees from 97 nations take care of 12 million Deutsche Bank customers, and more than half of our staff is based outside Germany. And we want to transform this diversity – the source of our strength – into creative and productive energy.

Business likes to use the term "diversity management" when describing this process. Generally, companies interpret the process as encouraging women, minorities and fringe groups. Deutsche Bank goes further: we want to create an organisational climate that will enable all employees to be successful, regardless of their background – and thus, ultimately to contribute to the success of our company.

We have established a "global diversity" programme to actively implement this process, and it is implementing a whole range of projects with clearly defined goals. For example, we have developed an equal opportunities staff recruitment and development programme, and we train our staff in cross-cultural discussion techniques. We have defined principles against harassment at the workplace. At Deutsche Bank in London, we have designated a prayer room which is open to all confessions.

Through our ISE (International Staff Exchange) programme, our employees are given the opportunity to experience first-hand a foreign country and culture, and thereby to broaden their horizons more than just professionally. We expressly encourage employees with similar interests to set up internal networks. These not only provide mutual support, but also open up new and better ways of understanding the company, its business and its customers, and of furthering professional skills. "Women in Business" is one example of a successful network, as is its American equivalent "Women on Wall Street".

In 1999, Deutsche Bank was awarded the accolade of TOTAL E-QUALITY for its equal opportunities approach to personnel policy. And even more important: the ratio of women earning non-tariff wages – i.e. in upper management – has increased from seven to just over 20 percent in Germany. That is still not enough by any means, but we are heading in the right direction. A globally active company such as Deutsche Bank clearly benefits economically from a personnel policy which focuses on diversity and tolerance. Any first-rate employer knows that it is counter-productive to ignore diversity, that it is in its best interests to acknowledge and encourage its creative potential. But isn't a worthy precept such as tolerance somehow devalued if it proves to be economically beneficial at the same time? On the contrary: it becomes even more appealing! As far back as the 17th century, the authors of the basic philosophical principles of the idea of tolerance, great minds such as John Locke, Baruch Spinoza and Samuel von Pufendorf, were not afraid to emphasise the very real benefit that tolerance could offer to those who exercise it. Does it really matter, ultimately, whether a tolerant attitude is motivated by philosophical, religious or utilitarian reasons? In my opinion, it is the result that matters – and this means that we need to attract the best talents to our team.

In 21st century commerce, analysts are rating corporations on their diversity concepts, which they consider of paramount importance. Many investors see a direct correlation between the creativity of a "diversified" team and income earned. The diversity factor therefore adds to the wealth of the company.

14   Deutsche Bank is a microcosm within a macrocosm. It is active across the globe and operates within the general conditions imposed by the local political system. This makes it imperative for political decision-makers to address issues of tolerance and diversity. It is becoming ever clearer that a successful diversity policy can greatly improve a location and give it a competitive advantage – and conversely, that the lack of a successful policy can harm a location. The apparent lack of debate on the issue in Germany is causing international companies to view the country with scepticism. For example, the government's Green Card plans – however good the idea might have been in principle – were ultimately unsuccessful at least in part because the international media kept raising the issue of xenophobia in Germany. The quality of the workplace is by no means the yardstick that determines whether we can offer skilled experts the quality of life that they demand for themselves and their families. Who would want to apply his or her internationally sought-after skills for the benefit of an economy that cannot even protect him or her from physical attack, let alone offer a climate of tolerance?

Thus, we want to use our strong commitment within the bank to stimulate social processes. This, too, is part of our understanding of our company's role as a corporate citizen: we aim to launch initiatives and exert formative influence.

Just how important it is to have a universal commitment to tolerance has become clearer than ever since September 11, 2001. The terror attacks in New York and Washington showed unmistakably just what people are capable of when they believe themselves to be the sole guardians of the truth, a delusion that renders them unwilling to, and indeed incapable of, communicating. However, communication is precisely what is required. A dialogue between cultures is the only way to avoid a battle of cultures. Such a dialogue can take place only on a foundation of tolerance. There must be a willingness on all sides to abide by rules acceptable to all, however different the interests and cultural characteristics of the parties involved. We must be able to endure the inherent tension in these relations in order to ensure that the world can become an open and civil society.

Tolerance is not some noble, remote objective of Deutsche Bank, nor is it an academic topic for speeches on high days and holidays. Rather, it is an ongoing daily attempt to debate, understand and resolve conflicts peaceably. Tolerance can, of course, mean conflict – but fought with arguments not armaments, and with the aim of striking a peaceful balance. The willingness to accept this precept must form the basis of co-existence on this planet. The limits of our tolerance are reached where there is no such willingness. Or, as Karl Popper said: "In the name of tolerance, we should claim the right not to tolerate intolerance".

Only in this way will we succeed in finding a sustainable concept of tolerance for the 21st century. By choosing tolerance as its theme for the year 2002, Deutsche Bank has made its commitment clear. And it has deliberately added to tolerance the notions of diversity and identity:

- Reality in the global village is determined by the diversity of cultures, religions, opinions, and lifestyles – in short: identities.
- Only when we have clearly defined our own person and identity are we able to understand other identities.
- The aim of this process of understanding is our mutual acknowledgement that the citizens of the global village all have equal standing and equal rights – and acknowledgement of the differences. This acknowledgement of different identities is the only way we can keep sight of fixed markers in a rapidly changing world. It is the only way we can secure open societies both internally and externally while integrating other ideas at the same time.

Active tolerance is the most important prerequisite for democracy. It is freedom's twin. Alfred Herrhausen, who in-

16 terpreted tolerance in the sense of openness, once said: "Freedom and openness – which go hand in hand – are not a gift. Mankind must fight for them, over and over again".

Rolf-E. Breuer
Spokesman of the Board of Managing Directors of Deutsche Bank. Chairman of the Board of Trustees of the Alfred Herrhausen Society for International Dialogue.

Born in 1937 in Bonn, Germany. Studied law in Lausanne, Munich and Bonn. Ph. D. in Law in 1967. Started his banking career at Deutsche Bank, Karlsruhe in 1966. Moved to the bank's Equities Department in Frankfurt in 1969. Became head of this department and an executive vice-president in 1974. Member of the bank's Management Board since 1985. Speaker of the Management Board since 1997.

WALTER HOMOLKA

THE END OF TOLERANCE?

Tolerance has never come by itself. Wars have broken out because tolerance has been denied, not because swords have been raised in its defence. Introduced with difficulty by idealistic rulers and convoluted philosophers purporting to offer enlightenment, it has always been imposed on the masses from above rather than welcomed by them as a cornerstone of human relationships. It is no coincidence that traditional wisdom claims we should "practice" tolerance. But who likes practising, anyway?

Tolerance is much more a burden than a release. Small wonder, then, that we labour under tolerance. Particularly since it demands that we accept moral decisions made by others and forces us to admit that we ourselves are prone to error. Few of us feel too happy with these imperatives; indeed, who among us likes to have our firmly entrenched views of the world shaken up, especially when things around us already seem to be falling apart? Tolerance has to keep proving its value in a world that has renounced Enlightenment. And it is not just a matter of the majority tolerating a minority; rather, it is a matter of acknowledging someone else's identity and granting him the respect owed to each individual in a pluralistic society.

But can tolerance work if there is no common ground for spiritual orientation and values? If a person cannot understand the insights of the Enlightenment, can he adhere to the rules that govern the Western world?

The Alfred Herrhausen Society has asked itself these questions and tried to come up with some answers. To this end, we asked a number of well-known authorities to present their thoughts on the principle of tolerance in modern times.

We were extremely curious to see how our authors would approach the seemingly evergreen principle of tolerance, since it was clear to us that each would come up with a different facet. The philosopher, the natural scientist, the novelist, the psychoanalyst, the conflict researcher, the theologian – we knew that each would have a different angle, so to speak. But we figured (if we ever really thought about it) that the topic itself would remain fairly immutable – tolerance, after all, is simply tolerance. Sure of himself and the world he lived in, Goethe once claimed: "Given the way I feel and think, it cost me nothing to let each man be what he was or even what he wanted to be".

However, from the moment we started preliminary discussions with our prospective authors, it became quite clear that any notion we might have harboured that tolerance was just tolerance was simply naïve. As the contributions of our authors show, blanket tolerance, the kind of tolerance which puts up with, or ignores, or simply endures more or less everything, can be stupid – and in the worst case, dangerous or even life-threatening.

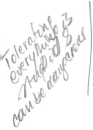

So – what is it that we want to, should or can tolerate? Especially these days, when the fears caused by globalisation are putting the most positive kind of tolerance at risk?

Our authors have pondered the origins of tolerance and traced them back to the world religions, an African tribal faith, literature, edicts, decrees and constitutions. In their rich and varied essays, they tell us how the principle of tolerance is practised – or not practised, as the case may be – in our daily relations with our peers, in our religions, in our cultures, in the context of our political and economic systems. They examine how crucifixes and headscarves are dealt with in German classrooms; what tolerance means on the streets of Armagh, New York or São Paulo; how tolerance can be applied in the natural sciences and in the realms of faith.

The writers of these essays have not shied away from the boundaries of tolerance. In the worst case, tolerance borders on blindness, indifference, ignorance. Even Nietzsche in his day was afraid that forbearance and patience sometimes served as superficial virtues. All of these "negative tolerances" – as well as the tolerance that seeks to deprive others of everything that makes them different – are no longer in keeping with the times. Quite simply – we can no longer afford them.

The opportunities provided through genuine co-existence in a global community are greater than ever before. But at the same time, the dangers we risk if we fail to grasp these opportunities are also greater than ever before. It is therefore crucial that we redefine the conventional concept of tolerance and find new ways to apply the regenerated principle. Only in this way can we make the best of our global future together.

At the end of this intellectual stroll among various views and ideas, we feel that the really important questions have been confronted and provocative ideas suggested: may they provide an impulse to go on thinking and discussing this issue.

Walter Homolka
Executive Director of the Alfred Herrhausen Society, Deutsche Bank, and head of the bank's Department of Cultural and Social Affairs.

Not having any opinions is the best way to achieve peace of mind.

GEORG CHRISTOPH LICHTENBERG

Georg Baselitz (*1938), untitled, 1998

TOLERANCE IN CIVIL SOCIETY

HARRIET MANDEL/ROBERT G. KAPLAN

CULTURAL COALITIONS IN NEW YORK CITY

A Case Study in Tolerance and Diversity

Dateline: New York City. Early in post-September 11 New York, the neighborhoods which constitute this city and make it one of the great global forces of human endeavour, revived with a determination and vigour never experienced before. These metropolitan communities were once again pulsing with life in every colour, shape, size, form, culture, ethnicity, nationality, religion, and life-style imaginable, and in a way which characterizes New York as a unique phenomenon of diversity. It is no exaggeration to say that the rich and vibrant complexity of humanity in New York is unparalleled anywhere in the world. New York gives diversity its fullest definition.

The unanimous response of New Yorkers to September 11 was the forceful determination to reclaim normalcy in the city. A crucial element of this normalcy is the assurance that our multiplicity of cultures can continue to live peacefully side by side. Never before has there been such appreciation of the vital need for mutual tolerance. Indeed, Michael Walzer's definition of tolerance as "the peaceful coexistence of groups of people with different histories and cultures" (Michael Walzer, *On Toleration*, Yale University Press, New Haven, 1997) has taken on profound significance as we bear witness to how cultural groups can clash, and the cataclysmic repercussions of what can happen when they do.

As New York began to record the unspeakable toll of the victims of the terrorist attack on the World Trade Center, it became increasingly clear that those lost reflected the diversity of the city in which the towers had stood. The victims in this horrific event came from more than sixty nations. While some were foreign nationals working for international corporations, many of those who perished were in fact among those "newest" arrivals who had made New York City their home.

America, the great social and political experiment of modern times, defines itself as a liberal, democratic, multi-racial and multi-ethnic immigration society. Those of us who are actively involved in the efforts to maintain a culture of pluralism have always recognized that our racial, ethnic and religious diversity is our challenge as well as our strength. At the beginning of the 21st century, America is becoming more diverse by the day, and in ways which increasingly test the boundaries of American cultural pluralism. We are moving from a nation descended from white Europeans and black Africans to one of a far more complex origin. America's increasingly diverse religious, racial and ethnic composition now includes Blacks from many different regions of the world, Hispanics from a wide range of Latin countries, Asians from across the Pacific Basin, and many more. Nowhere in our country is this rich diversity of people reflected more vividly than in New York.

NYC has historically been perceived as a "Mecca" for upwardly striving immigrant populations. During the past two decades, it has undergone an unprecedented demographic transformation. According to the 2000 census, in the previous ten years the population of the city grew by almost 10 percent, and the city accepted 1.2 million immigrants. "New" majorities have become the rule rather than the exception. In the 2000 census, white non-Hispanics made up only 35 per-

cent of the total of the city's population, down from 43 percent ten years earlier. Latinos now comprised 27 percent of
New York's population, making them the largest minority
group, and surpassing African Americans. Asian Americans,
once a small population, now comprised one out of every ten
New Yorkers.

The NYC Department of City Planning study entitled *The
Newest New Yorkers: 1995–1996: An Update of Immigration
to NYC in the mid-90s* indicates that while the city is home
to less than 3 percent of the U.S. population, it received 14
percent of all immigrants to the country. This increase in immigration was due primarily to the growth in refugee flows,
and a surge in those entering under the "diversity" provisions
of immigration law. To illustrate how America views itself as
an immigration society, and, moreover, one devoted to insur-
ing a diverse representation in our population, it should be
noted that the diversity provisions were enacted to increase
the flow of groups previously under-represented in the immigration stream to the United States. A look at the homelands
of immigrants to NYC shows that most came from the former Soviet Union and the Dominican Republic (18 percent
from each), China (10 percent), Jamaica and Guyana (5 percent each). Bangladeshi immigration to the city almost dou-
bled in the 1995–96 period, putting it in sixth place. Ireland,
in twelfth place in the early 1990s, dropped out of the city's
top 20 list. Ghana, Nigeria, and Egypt emerged as new "players" in the city's immigration scene.

Home to more than 180 different languages and ethnic
groups, by the year 2000 the city boasted one of the most
complex and diverse populations in the world. In Astoria
(Queens), there are schools where over 100 languages are
spoken. These students come from families which practice a
wide range of religions, cultures and traditions. It is evident
that the influx of these new immigrants to our nation poses a
multitude of new social, cultural, economic and political challenges. Indeed, within the context of these dramatic demo-

graphic shifts, New York's institutions and neighborhoods face a plethora of issues concomitant with the increasing diversification of the city's residents. These new demographic realities are significantly impacting on life in communities throughout the city in many different ways:

- The institutional level: There are increasingly complex and often conflicting demands being placed on policymakers and on the resources of government and political organizations, social service agencies, health care systems, educational institutions, businesses, housing agencies, and religious institutions. These institutions and organizations often lack the necessary knowledge and skills to effectively respond to and manage the evolving issues.

- Interactions between new and established populations: Communities become further strained as newly arriving groups move into neighbourhoods that are home to more established populations representing prior waves of immigration. In addition to the demands placed on community resources, tensions are exacerbated when prior immigrant groups perceive the newcomers as a threat to both their power base and their traditional way of life. This perceived threat is further magnified by the shrinking numbers of long-time city residents, as their populations become older, move up the economic ladder and either move to the more affluent suburbs or seek alternative housing to escape the changing character of their neighbourhoods.

- Interactions among and within new immigrant groups: Within the new immigrant groups themselves, serious tensions often arise. Mistrust and hostility emerge within populations who share a common cultural and/or geographic history; old, sometimes ancient, ethnic and religious prejudices may be transplanted from abroad into the new environment. Rivalries develop between the emerging and often competing leadership, and intolerance is further magnified by competition among and within groups for scarce resources. In addition, new leadership typically lacks the necessary experience and skills to effectively respond to issues of diversity.

It is important to recognise that the values of democracy, pluralism and tolerance which underscore the American constitutional tradition and which are so deeply rooted in our society are not necessarily considered values in many of the homeland countries of the immigrants. Yet they are the values which make America work. How can a society whose very fabric includes mutual respect and tolerance assimilate groups whose fabric does not, without causing those groups to abandon their cultural identities? How can people of so many diverse backgrounds tolerate each other? How can the residents of any given neighborhood in New York City live together harmoniously?

There are numerous institutions which play a key role in promoting integration in our society and in transmitting the American values. Among these institutions, voluntary associations perform an invaluable function. These informal associations have contributed immeasurably over generations to the integration of diverse immigrant groups into the mainstream of American life, to the forging of common bonds among the residents of any given community. To illustrate this kind of commitment, we will take a brief look at how one voluntary New York Jewish non-profit organization has developed grass-roots, community-based initiatives to address the challenge of sustaining peaceful co-existence in a large, diverse city.

According to its by-laws, the Jewish Community Relations Council of New York (JCRC), an umbrella organization for over 60 Jewish associations in the metropolitan area, is mandated to "encourage amicable relationships and mutual understanding and respect among the various groups in New York City" (paragraph d, article II) . To achieve this goal, the JCRC works to promote a more effective framework for

Jewish and non-Jewish grass-roots communal leadership to build effective coalitions and improve intergroup relations.

Coalition building is one of the most successful and time-tested strategies for strengthening relations between diverse religious and ethnic groups. Although it is extremely labour intensive, grass-roots neighborhood coalitions designed to address issues of mutual concern can provide the groundwork for further communal collaborative efforts. While dialogue has long been a useful tool for developing understanding, the concept of forming coalitions with the prime purpose of improving the day-to-day quality of life is relatively new. The immediacy of the goal is a strong incentive for the groups to work together. In attempting to identify and remedy specific issues which concern all involved, these grass-roots coalitions of ordinary people and communal leaders develop close working relationships. The participants feel that they are taking control of their lives, they experience a sense of empowerment and self-respect. In short, they feel that they are instrumental in shaping their own futures in a new country.

It is clear that finding common ground is essential in any attempt to confront racial, national and cultural barriers and break them down. Through participation, groups learn a lot about tolerance. Involvement and a common purpose help people to better understand each other's cultures and life styles. The more frequently the groups meet, and the more successful they are in achieving their goals, the greater the chance that they will succeed in breaking down stereotypes, reducing bigotry, parochialism and intolerance. Should a crisis ever arise, these groups already have a common history of cooperation and trust, and that makes it so much easier for them to solve the problems together.

One example of how functional grass-roots coalition building works is health care. Health care is an issue of great importance to all groups, identified by most community and faith-based organizations within the city as the foremost non-confrontational concern. The JCRC decided to use this as its entrance to community-based coalition building and founded the Northern Queens Health Coalition (NQHC). Established in 1994, the NQHC currently represents 60 member organizations; it serves communities throughout northern Queens and includes civic, religious and social service agencies representing the African-American, Chinese, Haitian, Indian, Italian, Jewish, Latino, Korean, Pakistani and Russian communities. Prior to 1994, the JCRC had realised that there was a strong need to develop a relationship between the growing Korean community and the well-established Jewish community of northern Queens. It initiated meetings between Korean and Jewish leaders, and it quickly became apparent that access to quality health care services and information was a major concern shared by both groups, and that this access was complicated by a host of factors related to cultural and language barriers. Working with the JCRC, Jewish and Korean community leaders created the coalition. Today, the NQHC has its own non-profit organization with a staff, a Board of Directors, and funding that allows it to tackle the problems of its diverse membership. Through the power of its diversity, the NQHC has been able to bring about real change in the quality of and access to health care for many populations who had previously been unable to utilize the complex health care systems.

It is difficult to describe in a few words how effective this coalition has been. Breast health care, for example, was almost non-existent among the many immigrant populations – they simply did not know about it or were unable to get it. Today, not only has it become available, but it is culturally sensitive in its delivery. Another example: a grant given to the coalition by New York State has enabled ten community-based agencies, each representing a different language, ethnic or cultural group, to provide free or inexpensive health insurance to their children. End-of-life care, so fraught with cultural and religious overlays and taboos, has been the subject of seminars and training. The coalition has prepared a health care guide for women that has been translated into six languages. The overall result has been not simply that health care for the immigrant groups is infinitely better than it was before, but that the groups have learned to work with each other, to trust each other, and to realise how much more they can achieve when they are united.

Bolstered by the success of the NQHC, the JCRC has now formed, or is consultant to, such neighborhood community-based initiatives as the Black-Jewish Congressional Coalition; The Greater Southern Brooklyn Health Coalition; The Staten Island Health Coalition; The Lower Manhattan Health Care Coalition; The Southern Westchester Child Health Plus Coalition; The Coalition for Far Rockaway; Project C.A.R.E./Crown Heights; Bronx Women Moving Our World; The Brighton Beach Coalition; Bridges to Brotherhood/Urban League, Aspira (Latino), Chinese-American; LaGuardia Community College-Queens Forum; NYCCCB (New York Center for Community and Coalition Building) Leadership Think Tank. In particular, the New York Center for Community and Coalition Building, operating under the auspices of the JCRC, serves as a vehicle to empower communal leadership within the diverse communities of NYC. The Center informs and trains policy and decision makers in the public and private sectors to effectively respond to the complex needs of a growing and increasingly heterogeneous population.

Coalition building has had a significant impact on the integration of immigrant populations into mainstream America. Coalition participants feel more American and more part of America. For all the reasons outlined above, they identify more as one large community. And they work together. This is exactly what happened in the aftermath of the World Trade Center tragedy. After September 11, with an established mechanism already in place, the JCRC was able to get in fast to defuse some of the extremely strained relationships between Muslim, Jewish and other communities in New York.

Within hours of the attack, the JCRC had established communication with leaders of the Arab American Family Support Center, the only social service center serving New York's Arab population and an institution with which the JCRC has a long and established working relationship.

In the weeks that followed, the JCRC maintained communication with Muslim leaders in New York and was called upon to help establish links between other communities and the Muslim community. It convened a meeting of communal leaders, representing the diversity of the city, at an Arab-American community organization, and is following up this meeting with the formation of several task forces. The JCRC also issued a statement against terror and hate, condemning the September terrorist attacks, and also deploring the ensuing anti-Muslim attacks which developed in local communities. This statement, published in a local community paper, as well as in six non-English papers in Arabic, Chinese, Korean, Russian, Spanish and Urdu, was signed by representatives of more than three hundred and fifty community faith-based and civic organizations.

The building of multi-cultural coalitions to achieve common goals, and the success of these enterprises, is living proof that diverse societies can live together peaceably and tolerate one another. The voluntary associations of New York City provide a working example of how such toleration can be achieved.

Harriet Mandel
Director of International Affairs for the Jewish Community Relations Council of New York.

Born in 1943 in New York. Earned a B. A. in Arabic and Islamic Studies, an M. A. in International and Public Affairs, and an advanced Certificate in Middle East Studies at Columbia University, New York. Member of several Middle East task forces, foreign policy consultant, lecturer on the Middle East, regular participant in public and background meetings with U. S. government officials and high-level diplomatic representatives.

Robert G. Kaplan

Founding Director of the Commission of Intergroup Relations and Community Concerns at the Jewish Community Relations Council of New York (JCRC).

Born in 1952 in New York. Attended Yeshiva Rabbi Chaim Berlin from 1981–1985, ordained as a Rabbi in 1985. Currently awaiting New York certification as a Conflict Mediator.

Liz Coffey

Getting Better All The Time

Diversity Issues in Business

A Conversation

Why would business have any interest in diversity in general and gender issues in particular?

To begin with, because the customer base is becoming increasingly diverse. Recent research in the United States has shown that 80 percent of buying decisions are either made directly by women or influenced by women. And while a lot of large companies were already aware of this, it came as a big surprise to quite a few others. So, if you have a customer base that is 80 percent female, but no women on your board or in senior management, you are losing out commercially by not cashing in on the strategic thinking capacity of representatives of your largest group of customers.

Couldn't a company simply employ a market research agency to find out what women want, and continue to keep all its top positions filled by men?

Market research could certainly supply some information, but that is an expensive way of doing things when you have talented women in your midst, women who have an innate understanding of the client base, women who could be promoted. And very often these days, the customer base wants to do business with a company that reflects its own composition. A company employing a management consultancy to conduct some work for them might ask the consultancy to reflect roughly the same gender and ethnic make-up as that of its own customer base. There are a number of different angles here: they want to understand the thinking of their customers through the consultants' thinking, to gain an impression of upcoming trends and customer requirements. Most big management consulting firms would have difficulties in finding senior women and ethnic minorities in large enough numbers to satisfy their customer demands.

Another major reason a company may find it in its own interests to become more diverse has to do with being considered an employer of choice. Companies are becoming increasingly aware that the people they have working for them are their most valuable asset, and the pool of extremely talented available people is getting smaller and smaller. So to attract and retain the best talent, you as a company have to demonstrate to the marketplace that you are a worthy organisation. If you are trying to attract diverse talent, if you are trying to recruit 50 percent women, for example, you have to demonstrate that you have the kind of culture that women will want to grow in, where they will thrive, where they can get promoted and climb to the top. Otherwise women will either not join you, or they won't stay.

Right now, unemployment in Europe and the United States is on the rise – can women afford to be that choosy? Can anyone?

Yes, I think that talented people still can. They follow the company ratings. These are based on worldwide surveys that profile companies and rate them in various categories. So a job hunter can find out a lot about the company she might be interested in joining. There are overall ratings – the ten or hundred best companies to work for – but also far more specific ratings which focus on particular features. So it's possible to find out which companies are best for ethnic minorities to work in, which companies are best for women. All of this is now public information, it's published by companies such as *Fortune* magazine; it's also available on the Web. And job-seekers often use it to decide with whom they want to interview. To return to your question – yes, really good people really do have a lot of choice; they can afford to shop around.

Are we talking mainly about women, or could we be talking about ethnic minorities or people with disabilities?

I'm talking about all underrepresented groups. And yes, there are surveys about the best place to work if you are disabled, the best place to work if you are an ethnic minority in the United States and so on. However, the women's issue gets the most attention, particularly in the United States and in the United Kingdom because there's been so much campaigning on that front for decades. And also because women make up more than 50 percent of the overall world population, so they are not exactly a minority population. They've had a louder voice over the years.

You appear to be talking very much about senior management, high senior posts. Does what you have been saying about ratings apply to middle management, to lower-ranking people?

Yes, it applies across the board. Young people fresh from university look carefully at the ratings. A few years ago, a large telecommunications company, Nortel Networks, realised that some of the women they were trying to recruit were turning them down in favour of a competitor. When Nortel looked into the reasons, they found out that it was because Nortel didn't have a mentoring program for women.

What exactly is that?

It's a program where a more senior person acts as a guide and informal advisor to a more junior individual in the company. And research has shown that companies with mentoring schemes are very good for the development of their mentees and their subsequent careers. The Nortel case simply indicates the level of sophistication that some 22-year-old United States college graduates possess: not only are they well aware of the company ratings, but they even know about the availability of mentoring programmes and take that into consideration.

You are American, you work in the United Kingdom. With regard to diversity, what differences do you see between the United States and Europe, or the United Kingdom in particular?

Well, the differences are considerable. Diversity as a business issue has moved along at a rapid pace in the United States. The United Kingdom is catching up slowly; Continental Europe, with the exception of the Scandinavian countries, is lagging behind the United States.

The United States is a very litigating culture, and one of the most interesting things that has happened in the history of diversity and business is that big companies have been sued by individuals and lost very publicly, and so massive payouts have been incurred.

For example?

Last year, Smith Barney, a brokerage house in New York, lost a major gender discrimination case against a group of women. It was a very public case, the press loved it, and the judge was female. As part of the settlement, the judge ordered that Smith Barney pay for a study by a research group called "Catalyst" into gender-in-business issues in the United States. Catalyst interviewed more than 1100 men and women at seven securities firms on Wall Street, and published their results in August of this year. The publication is called *Word on the Street*, and it is a fascinating exposé of gender issues in banking culture. So not only did Smith Barney have to pay huge damages, but they also had to pay for this piece of publicly available research.

Didn't Procter & Gamble get themselves out of a tricky gender situation recently?

Yes. About five years ago, Procter & Gamble realised that while their market was almost 100 percent female, women were not making it into the top ranks of the organization. As a result, they were failing to understand what their customers were thinking about their products and to project what their customers wanted. So they set up a mentoring scheme in which they reversed traditional roles and added a twist. Instead of having a more senior person act as guide or mentor to a more junior person, they arranged the system so that the junior women in the organization mentored the more senior men. This way, young women helped their older, more experienced male colleagues understand what kind of culture the men had inadvertently created, how that culture hindered women, what the women's needs were within P&G. This project was highly acclaimed, it got an Initiative of the Year Award by Catalyst, a very big accolade in the United States, and it has become well known.

Now that affirmative action is a thing of the past, are businesses motivated to set themselves quotas for minority groups?

Some businesses, certainly. Sociological research has shown that any group which represents less than 20 percent of the majority population – whether the group is black, white, male or female, physically disabled, whatever – that group has no voice. It cannot make itself heard. Add to that piece of information the fact that other major research in the United States has convincingly demonstrated that well-led diverse groups consistently outperform homogeneous groups by 15 percent – and you have a strong argument for self-imposed affirmative action.

Does the argument apply to companies across the board?

It applies particularly to organisations that are driven by research and development, for example to pharmaceutical companies or media companies or advertising companies, where you need a lot of creativity, a lot of innovation over a sustained period of time. These organizations need innovation at cutting-edge levels, so diversity actually adds in an obvious way to the bottom line for them. Not all companies have caught on to this yet, but word is slowly spreading.

You work with a number of different branches of industry, but you also work for the British government. Do you see significant differences between the private and the public sectors as far as diversity issues are concerned?

Overall, there is a lot of similarity in the way that they approach the issues, but there is a big difference in motivation. The private sector is primarily interested in commercial gain. So it looks for the kind of talent that will most benefit the organization; it looks at the composition of its customer base and ponders how that should be reflected in its own corporate composition to benefit organisational strategy and profit. To some extent, the reasoning applies to the public sector too, but you also have the added factor of fairness. The government wants to represent the composition of the general taxpaying public because it feels that that is the fair thing to do. And the public expects it. So, for example, if you are a British-born citizen of Indian descent, you will want the government to employ civil servants of Indian heritage in numbers reflective of the percentage populating the United Kingdom. There should be 50 percent women in the senior civil service. There should be 7 percent ethnic minorities in the senior civil service, because in the United Kingdom the overall population of ethnic minorities is approximately 7 percent. (Some cities have higher percentages of ethnic minorities; London, for example, has 25 percent, and cities like Bradford have a significantly higher percentage.) So the civil service is motivated to reflect the population, their customer base, because it is "the right thing to do."

In the past, you have been critical about the situation of women in the civil service. Has the situation changed?

Interestingly, on the gender diversity front, the British government is showing significantly higher numbers for senior women than is the private sector. In the government numbers are in the range of 10 to 12 percent at permanent secretary level, the equivalent of management board level in the private sector. In the FTSE 100 companies, women occupy less than 1 percent of executive director positions, and in the 200 to 250 listed top companies, only 3 percent of the executive directors are women. So the government is doing extremely well on that score, and I have to say that they are taking a lead with regard to ethnic minority diversity as well, trying hard in a variety of cutting-edge ways to move the numbers up. The head of the civil service has introduced a modernizing government agenda that includes increasing diversity; there are now stringent targets for diversity in top civil service positions. In 2000, there were 1.7 percent ethnic minorities in the senior civil service, but by 2004, there should be 3.2 percent. The way things are going now, there will probably be more.

Setting targets for yourself and then keeping track of your own performance is an excellent way to improve that performance. Moreover, you can make individual department managers accountable for the targets, so the whole system filters down. Within industry, some organizations have both qualitative as well as quantitative surveys. Through climate surveys or two-way performance management systems, a secretary can rate his or her boss and comment on his or her sensitivity to diversity issues. In some U. S. companies, a third of a person's bonus may depend on whether he or she has attained the diversity target, both on the quantitative and the qualitative measures.

Are there other significant ways in which a company which is committed to diversity can follow through on implementation?

There are a number of ways in which organizations have gone about becoming diverse. The first and most important one is to have senior people who are genuinely dedicated to the principle. They may believe in it for purely commercial reasons, but they have to really believe in it strongly because they have to be visible and vocal. They have to create a strategy which incorporates diversity into every area of the business; they have to keep everyone informed about whatever programmes have been introduced. Once they have incorporated diversity into the business, they have to set themselves targets, set their divisions and subdivisions targets. The targets must be ambitious but realistic. And then they have to shift their HR policies so that managers are given incentives, rewards, for achieving the targets. These are the kind of key things that leaders have to put into place to increase diversity in the workplace.

I've heard about the effectiveness of networking. How does that work?

The companies that have been most successful in incorporating diversity have been those which have created and fostered networks specifically for underrepresented groups. In the United Kingdom, one of the best examples is British Telecom, which is well-known for having a women's network, an ethnic minorities' network, a disabled network, and also a general business network in which everybody at BT is invited to participate. The reason BT networks are so successful has a lot to do with attitude. Networks often become moaning and complaining sessions, but this doesn't happen at BT. People get together in networks to discuss issues and come up with positive, workable solutions to problems. Then they figure out ways to implement those solutions. Sometimes the networks work together on issues which concern a number of them. Anyway, networking can be very productive, and more companies should encourage it.

There's another positive aspect to underrepresented group networking, and it goes together with mentoring. It used to be that networking was common in the majority population, the male population. Informal networks would spring up: a Friday-evening-at-the-pub network, a rugby network, a cricket network. The minority groups were left out. In these informal networks, friendships would grow. Over time a more senior man might get to know a more junior male colleague and think, "This guy has got real potential, I'll help him up through the organisation and mentor him, give him some tips, find him opportunities," and so on. Now, that kind of 'mentoring' used not to happen as much to women, ethnic minorities, disabled people, partly because they were kept out of the informal networks, partly too because senior men were not always happy about appearing to protect a younger woman. These days, however, underrepresented-group networking and formal mentoring programmes can overcome some of the difficulties. Not only are they extremely useful in enhancing the careers of the minority group members, but they can actually help the company by improving the information flow up and down the line. Through these new networks and mentoring, instead of just moving from top to bottom, good ideas may spread faster from the lower to the higher levels of decision-making.

In conversation with Susan Stern.

Elizabeth (Liz) Coffey

Leadership coach at The Change Partnership, an executive coaching consultancy.

Born in 1959 in New York. Studied English and psychology at Wellesley College. Coach for senior executives of the FTSE-100 companies and public sector organisations. Leader of diversity development projects on gender, ethnicity, disability, organisational and national culture.

Selected publications: *The Changing Culture of Leadership: Women Leaders' Voices (co-author in 1999) – a study on women leaders in the UK.*

DANIEL GOEUDEVERT

NOTHING FROM NOTHING

Tolerance and Competition

People who stay in one spot
are nothing but rational oysters.
Friedrich Schlegel

Pluralism and tolerance, mobility and flexibility, openness
and transparency are universally heralded as the new requirements, the key skills, in a globalised world. If, however, you
want to find out more about what they actually involve and
mean in practice, the results are generally disappointing. If we
brush aside the buzzwords, we discover that most of us live
"in one spot", that we have remained what Schlegel once
described as nothing but – more or less – rational oysters.
Immobile and inward-looking, rigid, tight-lipped, and tor-
mented by fears of loss, we hide our "pearls" away without
realizing that the value of these riches can only truly be appreciated through the eyes of others and in dialogue with them.

   Let's take a closer look at one of our most precious facul-
ties: thought. The ancient Greeks – Socrates, Plato and Aristotle – knew that it could be developed only in and through
discussion, that thought therefore required difference as a
necessary foil. As a result, wise people throughout history
have almost always considered fellowship, empathy, charity,
compassion, solidarity, fraternité, or whatever name we might
give this source of community, an essential element of what it
means to be human. The French philosopher Gabriel Marcel
once wrote that thought is always oriented towards differ-

ence, "it is a longing for what is different." Nowadays, however, there would seem to be a severe shortage of this kind of longing and therefore of thought itself. Wherever we turn, people are finding it difficult to confront the unfamiliar – whether it be another culture or religion, or even the opposite sex – with agreeable, but self-confident distance. The inquisitive outwardness that makes dialogue and joint action possible and supplies the raw material for thought is now in danger of being replaced by a sometimes anxious, sometimes aggressive inwardness. At best, in its defensive form, this kind of inwardness makes us oysters; at its worst, it creates madmen and killers.

If this observation is true, then the future is likely to be even more problematic than the extremely difficult present that confronted us long before the murderous attacks in New York and Washington. Encounters with the unfamiliar, concrete experiences of difference, incongruities and inequalities will continue to increase, not despite, but because of globalisation. Today huge rifts already run through societies, both nationally and internationally. I often use a simple image, which stems from Manfred Max-Neef, a member of the Club of Rome, to make the complexity of the situation clear. Imagine the world as a small settlement with 1,000 inhabitants. This village is home to 564 Asians, 210 Europeans, 86 Africans, 80 South Americans and 60 North Americans. Of the 1,000 inhabitants, 310 are Christians, including 189 Roman Catholics, 87 Protestants and 34 Eastern Orthodox; 183 inhabitants are Muslims, 134 Hindus, 60 Buddhists, 36 Jews, 54 animists, and 223 have no religious affiliation. A little more than half the population are women.

At a first, cursory glance, our village might make rather a good impression – a pluralistic, multicultural and multi-religious community. If you take a closer look at its inner constitution, however, you find that only 60 inhabitants own more than 50 per cent of the entire wealth; the other 940 have to share the rest between them. Furthermore, 500 inhabitants suffer from hunger, 600 live in slums, and 700 cannot read or write. And as we know, the picture is also not particularly rosy when it comes to mutual respect, to tolerance and generosity, to participation and equal opportunity.

This place is exactly what we describe as the global village – some with high hopes, others with great concern, but almost all without regard for cultural and historical differences. When we speak of the global village, however, we do not primarily mean the One World for which we all bear a common responsibility, but a world market in which we must all participate as economic players and whose challenges we must face, whether we wish to or not. This is what companies and what we as individuals have to be "fit" to deal with – not a particularly easy feat for oysters. Experts recommend the most diverse fitness courses – "international competence", "self-coaching", "change management" – and attempt to "open" us up so that we can become "tolerance and pluralism-capable", as it is so elegantly described in German.

Although the economy has attained a dangerous dominance over all other aspects of life, I am convinced that economic activity has a civilising and humanising potential. The marketplace has always been a centre of dialogue, of negotiation, of compromise. It can equalise conflicting interests, even promote peace, and because it presupposes equality before the law, where tyranny reigns it can only function in a restricted form, generating strong pressures for democracy.

Firms that are active in more than one region also have a strong interest in breaking down patterns of prejudice and overcoming social differences, and they are even less likely to accept harsh restrictions on, and the exclusion of, potential market participants. In order to increase their sales, they need stable social structures and a preferably increasing number of free and prosperous consumers whose demands and needs they attempt to understand and satisfy. This process may initially involve purely economic, commercial considerations, but it will also foster other, unintended values and leave its mark on the economy as a whole as well as on society. We only have to think, for example, of the Daimler-Chrysler group: during the apartheid era, its South African subsidiary was the first business to employ and train black workers in substantial numbers and thereby subvert the principle of racial segregation.

Naturally, it would be just as easy, probably far easier, to find negative examples and to criticise the havoc caused by blinkered economic self-interest. The dividing line is very fine, and the extremes are very close together. Yet economic activity in itself is not the problem. Business is merely a means to an ends, which we have to define ourselves as well as the rules to be followed in pursuit of these ends. We cannot rely on the frequently cited "invisible hand". Although the founders of liberal economics believed very strongly in its beneficial effects and today's neo-liberals still roll the phrase out to attack any form of regulatory intervention, the "hand" is quite simply invisible because it does not exist.

The concept of the self-regulating market is based upon the absurd notion of a form of human equality unrestricted by dependencies or external influences. Because the same "simple human being" is supposedly found within each and every one of us, there is no need for special regulations; any intervention merely disturbs the natural harmony. Laissez faire, laissez aller! But there are problems with this interpretation, as both past and present experiences – for example, with the global village outlined above – clearly demonstrate. You only have to ask a woman, or an African, or an Afghan, what they think about natural equality, and you will find that the manifest inequalities of real life lead to new oppression when freedom is not structured by rules: the weak are subjugated by the strong, the poor by the rich, women by men. The equality upon which freedom is based is not determined by nature, but by culture. It is not intrinsic, but extrinsic: a moral precept, a human right that demands constant effort on our part – even if it is in our own self-interest.

48   However, is the market, business, really the appropriate medium for establishing such equality? Shouldn't it be the other way around? Shouldn't equality first be put in place to allow something like a market to develop, a forum whose very functioning depends on the mutual trust of all its participants, who meet as "equals"? Their equality, however, has nothing in common with the uniformity generated when goods are manufactured using standardised processes. The equality we mean here proves itself, as Jean Cocteau once put it, first by accepting, possibly even resolving contradictions, not by suppressing differences. It is therefore based on tolerance.

This is an equivocal concept. Tolerance is undoubtedly one of the fundamental virtues of democracy, but it is a strangely ambivalent force that occurs in two varieties: in a solid and in a decorative form. Being tolerant, allowing others to be themselves, respecting others and their origins and backgrounds always means refusing to tell others what to do and not wanting to influence them to follow one's own ideas and for one's own advantage. Tolerance calls for dialogue aimed not at achieving a common stance, but at communicating and explaining differences. This presupposes mutual recognition, which can be terminated, but which first and foremost prohibits any form of dogmatism: curiosity is its guiding principle, not competition.

There is, however, the other side of the coin, the decorative variety of tolerance that entails no commitment and seems to blend wonderfully with smug complacency while making it possible to attach an aura of virtue to one's own passivity. Tolerance would appear to be booming in this second, "light" version, which can ultimately be so tolerant that it even tolerates its antithesis, intolerance. Naturally, all foreigners are tolerated in Germany, provided they adapt, in other words, change and accept German culture as their *Leitkultur*, their leading culture. Naturally, we support women's equality in the world of work and would also tolerate a woman as boss, provided nobody calls upon us men to change or even give up our own jobs. Enlightened opinion often proves to be nothing more than cynical indifference, a mask.

I believe that a certain amount of scepticism is in order now that the cause of tolerance has been taken up by business and is being vociferously advocated by its opinion-shapers. "Tolerance marketing" has really taken off: diversity, openness and internationality are now seen as competitive advantages in the age of globalisation. Accordingly, it has become an important element of business correctness for firms to acquire the relevant flair and, for example, to ensure that boards have international representation. Since I have been a member of such a board, I could describe the many advantages, the increase in insights and ideas that can ensue from a dialogue between people with different origins and backgrounds. However, my experience has also taught me that diversity alone has no intrinsic value. In fact, it can even lead to the opposite of tolerance if it is not coached and guided. Real tolerance – of the solid variety – is a process. It is not enough to simply bring together people from different cultures, of different ages and sexes. The important thing is how these people treat one another and others, for example, their employees and their customers.

Let us imagine a block of flats. The ground floor is inhabited by Turks who live largely according to the rules of the Koran. The clothes they wear, the food they eat and the music they listen to are all very Turkish. The first floor is home to Hungarians. They have large numbers of visitors and enjoy partying into the early hours. On the second floor live a friendly, but reserved English family whose kitchen smells of dinner first thing in the morning. In the last flat, on the third floor, live a group of Germans who spend a long time watching television on Saturdays, eat roast pork on Sundays, and do not have much time for loud, lively parties. If they wish to develop a sense of community, the first thing the tenants must practise and exercise is acceptance. In other words, they must respect the fact that the other tenants are the way they are and at least make allowances for how others live by examining their own behaviour to see if it might disturb their neighbours and make minor adjustments accordingly. Knowing each other is a prerequisite for achieving this. Tolerance is not dispassionate. It turns into energetic assistance in emergency situations. If there is a flood, if a fire breaks out in the building, active solidarity is required. The tenants then suddenly find themselves dependent on one another, have to help one another – and are all the better able to do so, the better they know one another. The Hungarians will then put down their glasses in the middle of their party to warn the English, who they know always go to bed early, about the flood or fire. Acceptance and mutual respect are the prerequisites for this kind of solidarity-based tolerance, out of which understanding and empathy can also grow – although they need not. After all, tolerance should not be misunderstood as some kind of "do-gooder event" or even as a training area for indifference. I can neither expect others to accept me unconditionally in all I say and do, nor must or should I tolerate everything others do. No, enlightened tolerance has and sets limits, first and foremost in the form of self-restraint: putting someone else's interests before your own, making allowances, considering whether and how your actions affect those around you. And this self-restraint does not spring from selflessness, it is not purely altruistic in nature, but is based on social reason, on the realisation that my well-being is very much dependent on the recognition of others and that both present and future are only worth living with mutual respect.

Yet can this concept of tolerance become the central element of a corporate culture? Can it be reconciled with business interests, hierarchical management structures, and employees' "dependent" status? I believe that this is possible, but have yet to see examples. Under the prevailing conditions of competition, in my view, there is no room for tolerance. Where all errors are punished and the smallest delay is avoided, where every mistake is viewed as failure, where competitors are ferociously resisted, where victory alone counts and the winner takes all, pluralism and tolerance, openness and transparency are little more than propaganda slogans. Only if we succeed in developing new competitive models that no longer understand competition as rivalry, but as co-operation, will talk of tolerance be filled with meaning. This concept would then describe ethical, responsible conduct not only towards our social environment, but also towards employees and customers, and it would cease to be mere public relations. By necessity, responsible conduct would also include a deceleration of and self-restraint in business activities. Exercising tolerance, learning from mistakes, and understanding others take time and involve making allowances for exhaustible people and resources. Nonetheless, I am certain this "investment" would be worthwhile.

winner takes all

However, investing in the future in this way calls for courage, which in turn presumes an outlook that forms the essence of what I call tolerance. This ambitious attitude was once defined as follows by Alfred Herrhausen, who also personified it in an exemplary way: "We must say what we think, we must do what we say, and we must be what we do." I know how difficult that is to achieve, and how much more difficult it is to keep it up. But I also know that the effort pays off.

Daniel Goeudevert
Auto industry executive. Vice-President of Green Cross, a foundation promoting environmentally friendly and culturally protective tourism in the developing world.

Born in 1942 in Reims, France. Studied literature at the Sorbonne. Switched careers from teaching to management in the auto industry. Headed Citröen, Switzerland, 1971–74; Renault, Germany in 1975; and Ford-Werke, Germany,

when winner takes all – pluralism, tolerance, openness, & transparency are nothing more than prop.

52   1981–1989. Appointed Member of the Management Board of Volkswagen Group (VW) in 1989. Became head of VW global brand and Deputy Chairman of VW Management Board in 1993. Initiated the management school project CAMPUS (Dortmund).

Selected publications: *Wie ein Vogel im Aquarium. Aus dem Leben eines Managers* (1996); *Mit Träumen beginnt die Realität. Aus dem Leben eines Europäers* (1999); *Der Horizont hat Flügel. Die Zukunft der Bildung* (2001).

PETER C. GOLDMARK JR.

WE ARE ALL MINORITIES NOW

Author's note: This article is written with deep gratitude and indebtedness to Amin Maalouf, whose brilliant work Les Identités Meurtrières *has strengthened, influenced and advanced my own thinking. To cite him in a footnote is not sufficient, although direct quotes are of course attributed. So I have chosen to mention his name here and to pay tribute to the lucidity and generosity of his thought. Had I his permission, I would have listed him as co-author of this piece, or at least as co-inspirer.*

In Kosovo, in Ireland, in Sumatra, in the Middle-East, in Angola, in Chechnya, in the Congo, throats are slit every day as lives are taken in the name of communal hatred. This is human practice of long standing. It may once have been an evolutionary trait which gave one tribe a competitive advantage over another.

At the same time we see around the world trends of convergence and even homogenization as the same stores, products, songs, movies, vehicles, fashions and body decorations sweep the globe. This is the contemporary culmination of the most sweeping human cultural and economic impulse to have appeared on this planet: Western technology and systems of economic activity and marketing.

We live at a moment in history when the intersection of these two trends – one as old as human history itself, the other perhaps a century and a half old – makes the crossroads at which we stand uniquely fateful. This is so for three reasons: because the fighters on behalf of the ancient hatreds are acquiring access to weapons of mass destruction made possible by Western technology; because the tidal wave of Western-inspired globalization generates reaction, resistance, and intolerance as well as admiration, envy and imitation; and because the present economic pattern of Western civilization, it becomes increasingly clear, will lead to environmental and consequently economic disaster.

An important step is to identify and recognize some of the mechanisms by which the deadly virus of communal hatred and intolerance is transmitted. One mechanism is the terrifying ease with which we generalize descriptions and assign blame. Maalouf writes:

> *Because it is so easy, we group people who are enormously different under the same catch-all labels, and because it is so easy, we attribute to them crimes, collective action, and collective opinions: "the Serbs massacred...", "the English pillaged...", "the Jews seized...", "the Blacks burned...", "the Arabs refuse..." Mindlessly we issue judgments on this or that people, whom we call "hard-working", "skillful" or "lazy", "sensitive", "dark", "proud" or "stubborn", and sometimes this all ends in blood. ... It seems to me important that each one of us realize that these terms are not innocent, and that they perpetuate prejudices that have proven throughout history to be perverse and deadly.[1]*

The media contribute to this crime of generalization. Some newspapers and occasionally television make a strong effort to avoid it; but most contribute to it, knowingly or unknowingly:

> *In a second mechanism at work, the forces of globalization reinforce the hardening of identity, and consequently often of intolerance. "There is no doubt that accelerating globalization provokes, in reaction, a strengthening of the need for identity. And a strengthening as well, because of the existential anxiety that accompanies these brutal changes, of the hunger for spirituality. Only religious adherence brings, or claims to bring, a response to both these needs... But it seems to me that in the rising tide of religion there is more than a simple "reaction" [to globalization]. Communities of believ-*

ers begin to function as planetary tribes – I say "tribes" be-
cause of their fierce sense of identity, but I say "planetary" as
well because they transcend geographic frontiers. Adherence
to a faith that transcends national, racial, and social cate-
gories will appear to some to be a way of becoming universal.
Adherence to a community of believers will thus be in one
sense the most global belief, the most universal particularism;
or perhaps it would be better to say the most tangible, the
most "natural", the most rooted universalism.[2]

These "planetary tribes" live in polarized worlds of believers
and non-believers, whether they solidify in response to globalization, or from endogenous causes, or both; and there we
find intolerance, fanaticism, and the brutal revisionism that
breeds and justifies hate and genocide. And where we find
mindless globalization that grants no respect and attributes
no value to other cultures, or to practices and attitudes that
are at variance with those of the West, there we find also a
kind of intolerance. The economic and cultural tidal wave of
globalization rolls across traditional communities with a
blind indifference that attacks and destabilizes their value systems, and is itself often expressed in the kind of brutal revisionism that justifies prejudice and feelings of superiority.

And that is why the cycle of revenge and slaughter continues.

The blind fingers of history scrabble relentlessly, moving
from bead to bead on the dark rosary of violence. If you begin with a red bead, then there must follow a black bead of revenge and death. If you begin with a black, then a red bead of
bloodshed must come next. But no matter where you start,
you will shortly accept and then assert that the universe is
composed only of red and black beads, whichever cause you
may exalt and whichever values you may denigrate. And no
matter where you start, the inexpiable cycle of communal hatred continues, and you will be trapped in the fatal dance of
polarization, revenge, and violence – black followed by red,

red by black, death followed by revenge, revenge by more
bloodshed.

To sustain oneself in this cycle is psychically impossible for
most humans without taking refuge in a superordinate belief
system of one kind or another. Religion, traditionally, is the
most effective type, although there have been powerful secular examples in the past century, including Nazism and communism. To pursue the bloody cycle of slaughter, vengeance
and purifying self-justification is not possible for most humans outside an intolerant belief system that polarizes all,
permits all, justifies all, and forgives all.

But when the mouths of men are full of hate, it is rarely the
voice of God we hear.

This may appear a gloomy picture of who we are and what
awaits us. But I do not believe that it is.

Is our future pre-ordained? If there is one lesson of history,
it is that the future is open. It is not what we think it will be,
and it is not certain. Predictions, whether rosy or gloomy,
have usually proven to be wrong. If the future is open, then
generous understanding and intelligent, adaptable action are
what we should seek.

Maalouf urges skepticism as a basic tool for all of us:

> *Skepticism is without doubt one of the critical words of our
> time. Skepticism toward ideologies, toward rosy tomorrows,
> skepticism toward politics, toward science, toward reason,
> toward modernity. Skepticism toward the idea of progress
> and toward practically everything in which we believed
> throughout the twentieth century – a century of enormous
> accomplishment, without precedent since the dawn of time,
> but a century also of unpardonable crimes and dashed
> hopes. Skepticism also toward all that presents itself as
> global, worldwide, or planetary.[3]*

Maalouf dreams as well of a world where religion will no
longer be the active agent in so many lethal mixtures of *dicta*
and attitudes. This is a difficult but important thought:

I do not dream of a world where religion has no place, but of a world where the need for spirituality will be dissociated from the need for belonging. Of a world where humans, while remaining attached to their beliefs, to a denomination, to moral values ultimately inspired by a Holy Book, will no longer feel the need to enroll in the army of their co-religionists. Of a world where religion will no longer serve as the glue for ethnic war. To separate church from state will no longer be enough; it will be just as important to separate religion from identity. And equally, if we wish to prevent this amalgam from feeding fanaticism, terrorism and ethnic wars, it will be necessary to satisfy the need for identity in other ways.[4]

To this I add a different note of hope. I call it the "minority sensibility", and I mean by that term to describe a consciousness that is both subtle and powerful, that is spreading without many of us realizing it, and that has not existed before in the human adventure on this planet.

Since the beginning of history, all human activity, and human thought about our world, our context, and our activity, can be considered to have taken place within what I would call the "arena of consciousness". By that I mean the world we experience and imagine, with boundaries defined and limited by our actual experience plus what our knowledge and imagination can build on top of that.

For most of the few million years during which humans have performed on this planet, the "arena of consciousness" was the world of the hunter-gatherer tribe – a group of perhaps 15–40 individuals, inhabiting a large territory within and at whose boundaries they occasionally encountered other people. These other people usually looked like themselves. When they did not, and sometimes even when they did, they often fell into warfare with them, and in the process stereotyped and demonized them.

Human history then moved to the period of agricultural

58   settlements. Again, the majority of people encountered in these settlements, and in most neighboring ones as well, looked and talked and prayed in similar ways. There followed in a jumbled fashion feudal holdings, city states, and then in the seventeenth century the arrival in the West of the nation state. In each of these arenas of consciousness, there was an ethnic majority that was dominant. That means that for the first few million years of human history, the majority of human beings grew up thinking, living, and acting with the mental equipment and cultural habits of ethnic majorities.

And then during the twentieth century, humans jumped another electron ring in their arena of consciousness. The boundaries of our arena of consciousness expanded to include the entire planet.

When did this happen? For some, it may have happened with those dramatic and beautiful pictures of the earthscape taken from the moon. For others it may have happened with the arrival of regular "world news". For still others, the birth of the United Nations or the coming of age of the multinational corporation may have had something to do with it. Whatever the particular moment, a world that can watch *Dallas,* the fall of the Berlin Wall, a lone demonstrator stopping a tank column in Tiananmen Square, and the destruction of the World Trade Center by the hundreds of millions across the planet is truly operating within an arena of consciousness that is global.

And that means that for the first time in history, those of us for whom the arena of consciousness is global imagine ourselves working, living, travelling, and interacting in a context where no single group constitutes an ethnic majority. Whatever ethnic group we may identify with or belong to, that ethnic group is a minority in the global arena of consciousness. I believe the consequences of this change in the underlying mindset may be both powerful and hopeful.

We are just at the beginning of this discussion about tolerance, about identity, about globalization, and about the implications of the fact that now we are all minorities.

The future is open, and little is certain.
The stakes are enormous.

We must search within ourselves, we must think generously, we must react prudently and gently, and we must empathize with daring imagination. We must be respectful and measured in the assertion of our own beliefs, and passionate in the rejection of hate and prejudice in all its forms. Above all, we must listen with compassion and reflection. We must listen to new voices, and we must listen to old voices in new ways. All violence, in whatever form and for whatever cause, must now be suspect. We must bend ourselves to this task, because we do not have as much time as we once thought we did. And we must approach these sensitive subjects carefully and thoughtfully, because if we rush and do not devote to it as much time as it requires, then we will achieve nothing.

NOTES

1 Maalouf, Amin, *Les Identités Meurtrières*, 1998, Paris, p. 29. Unless indicated otherwise, citations are translated from the French by PG.

2 *Ibid.*, pp. 106–7.

3 *Ibid.*, p. 111.

4 *Ibid.*, p. 110.

Peter C. Goldmark Jr.
Chairman and CEO of the *International Herald Tribune*.

Born in 1940 in New York. Graduated in Government from Harvard College in 1962, Magna Cum Laude. President of The Rockefeller Foundation, 1988–1997. Senior Vice-President of the Times Mirror Company, 1985–1988. Executive Director of The Port Authority of New York and New Jersey, 1977–1985; Director of the Budget of the State of New York, 1975–1977; Executive Assistant to the Mayor of New York, 1971.

Ian Buruma

THE LIMITS OF CULTURAL TOLERANCE

A Conversation

Is it meaningful to talk about tolerance in the context of inter-cultural relations?

Oh yes, it's clearly meaningful. Tolerance is a notion that can be applied to different kinds of confrontations between cultures and habits, confrontations which take place within a given country – you could call them domestic – and confrontations between countries. Domestic confrontations are between majority culture behaviour and the cultural behaviour of minorities who are part of the same society. In France, for example, everybody who goes to a public school has to conform to secular rules. Now this does not go down well with those Muslims who insist that their daughters wear headscarves. In many Western countries, first generation Muslim fathers from places such as Turkey or Morocco are frightened of losing control over their families, and particularly over their daughters who are born in the West and adopt Western customs and habits. These fathers are often stricter than they might have been if they had stayed in their country of origin. At any event, the situation leads to clashes between fathers and daughters – if the father tries to impose an arranged marriage, for example. Occasionally, well-meaning social workers appear on the scene when such conflicts break out, and side with the father – in the name of protecting the cultural rights of minorities. Now here, I think, there is a limit to domestic tolerance.

On the one hand, we should, of course, show tolerance towards the cultural habits of minorities. But on the other, we should extend to everyone within a Western country the civic freedoms that every citizen of a Western democracy should enjoy, including the right to choose a marriage partner. In other words, I believe the law of the land should always apply to those who live in that country. It is a big mistake to have separate rules that apply only to minorities. This was a mistake made in India, for example. Some Muslims demanded special religious laws that would allow them to have several wives. But as soon as these laws were approved to appease the leaders of the Muslims, the leaders of the Hindu majority demanded their own religious laws. So in fact, this "tolerance" towards a minority group culture increased rather than resolved tensions. However, when cultural practices do not conflict with the law, when Sikh bus drivers wear turbans instead of the regulation caps on London buses, for instance, I don't see a problem and we can easily afford to be tolerant. All in all, though, I think it is best to take the law of the land as the final arbiter in these things. So, for example, I don't think that Bavarian schools should be allowed to hang crosses on classroom walls. Germany is a secular state and I don't think secular schools should identify themselves directly with a particular religion. But I see no problem with individuals wearing crosses or headscarves.

The notion of "Leitkultur", of a so-called defining or dominant culture, has been making waves in Germany recently, and is part of an ongoing debate. If I understand you correctly, you would agree that outsiders, immigrants, should go along with the prevailing culture of the country?

In the end, I believe that people should be encouraged and given every opportunity to adopt the language and the culture of the country they are living in, without necessarily having to discard their own ways ... I don't think it's a good idea to encourage separateness, to encourage people to stay within their communities, because it narrows their options and liberties. Second generation immigrants are born in a country whose culture they are then encouraged not to follow. So I do think that immigrants should be educated in the language and the culture of the native population, and then if they choose to have extra classes in their minority culture ... well, of course, that's fine.

Now the problem is somewhat different when it comes to relations between countries rather than between domestic minorities. There is no way to impose common rules, common habits on sovereign countries. Western countries may be opposed to practices such as genital mutilation, and certainly international organizations and NGOs can voice their opinions on such matters, but a ban on female circumcision is obviously not something that one government can impose on another. But here again, I am always very sceptical of any school that claims each country has its own culture – for example, a particular set of political arrangements or ideas about civil liberties that have grown out of Western history – and that this culture cannot be applied to other countries where the culture is quite different. I am sceptical, because who defines a culture? All too often, it is the rulers of a particular set of political arrangements, who justify their rule by proclaiming their way of doing things as "the native culture". This is particularly true in countries where institutions are not based on any kind of common consent guaranteed through elections or free public opinion, but where the rulers are despots. Despotic rulers tend to use culture as a justification for the continuation of their rule.

I think it's important to at least try to separate culture from politics, however much politics may be influenced by culture.

Let me give a specific example. In 1945, after Germany had been finally defeated, the Americans came to Japan feeling that it was not enough to just introduce democratic institutions – they felt the whole culture had to be changed, because the culture was supposedly too feudal. One of the ways that democracy was to be introduced in Japan was with a brand new liberal and democratic constitution which would replace the old and less-than-liberal constitution – well, a constitution that had been vague enough to allow Japan to institute imperial authoritarianism. Now, the more conservative Japanese lawyers who were consulted on this, and the conservative Japanese politicians, who were by no means fascists, but who were very distrustful of democratic institutions, they all believed that authoritarian politics were suited to Japan. They'd grown up believing this, and after all, they were the elite. And they argued that the new proposed constitution was alien to Japanese culture, that it would not be understood, it would lead to chaos, whereas the old constitution was, in their view, in tune with Japanese culture. Now in fact, the old constitution had indeed been written by the Japanese, but it had been written in the late 19th century and had been copied from the Prussian constitution. So the old constitution did not exactly represent ancient Japanese culture. And the interesting thing was that many of the foreigners, the Americans who shared the reservations of the Japanese conservatives, were experts on Japan, they supposedly knew Japanese culture well. So they opposed the new constitution, while Japanese public opinion and Japanese liberals were very much in favour of the more American-style, more democratic constitution.

So one has to recognize that culture is never monolithic and should never be used as a justification for maintaining political institutions that reduce people's choices. This same situation comes up again and again. It came up at the time of Tiananmen in China, when the world was wondering whether democracy is possible in China. Well, of course, members of the Chinese Communist Party said, still say,

"No, we need authoritarianism, because otherwise people don't understand, … without firm authority, you get chaos, disorder and so on. It is not in the Chinese tradition." Many experts on China in the West echo that opinion, as do many businessmen. The businessmen often do it for self-serving reasons because they get on well in an authoritarian country with a central power, it makes it easier to do business. But one should be very suspicious of what the experts say. None of them can really explain why democracy is doing so well in Taiwan. In fact, Taiwan is very embarrassing to people who defend the "school of Asian values" and they have to come up with other arguments. Taiwan is so small, they say. But what about India, then?

So I think that using culture, cultural tolerance, as an argument for maintaining the political status quo should be viewed with great suspicion. When it comes to the forms of political institutions and social habits and so on, obviously there are differences, it would be wrong to try to make them all the same … But again, I don't think the argument that people should be given civil liberties and a maximum of choice in their personal lives and in the way their countries are run means that one is advocating that everybody should become like an American or that every government should be based on the Westminster model. There are very many different ways in which these things can be done.

You obviously feel strongly that people everywhere regardless of their country and culture have a basic right to civil liberties and personal choice. Women make up about half of the population of the world, but in many countries, they have far fewer of these basic rights than men have.

Of course I believe that all individuals regardless of gender should have equal rights and liberties. But what is desirable is not always practicable. It is obviously not within the brief of Western countries to impose on other countries these things

Receipt

Cheque Processing Times
For information on cheque processing times, see table overleaf.

Date/time	: 30 DEC 2003 12:53:58
Credit to Account	: 0294/641703117
Cash/Cleared Funds :	************ Credited
Cheque Amount :	************
Flex Chq Amount :	************ £28.63
Reference Number	: 0294/A007G 0112

Nationwide Building Society

Banking | Credit Card | Insurance | Investments | Loans | Mortgages | Pensions | Savings

Cheque Processing Times

1. FlexAccount with a chequebook OR a FlexAccount cheque paid into any Nationwide Account

Mon	Tues	Wed	Thur	Fri	Sat	Sun
CH			£			
	CH			£		
£		CH				
	£		CH			
		£		CH		
					CH	

2. Savings Account OR FlexAccount without a chequebook

Mon	Tues	Wed	Thur	Fri	Sat	Sun	Mon
CH			£				
	CH			£			
£		CH					
	£		CH				
		£		CH			
					CH		£

Key: CH – Cheque deposited   £ – Available for withdrawal

Please add an extra day for every additional Bank Holiday.

For withdrawal purposes, cheques paid in on a Saturday will be treated as if paid in on the following Monday.

FlexAccount cheques paid into any Nationwide account will be available for withdrawal after 3 working days (use table 1).

Although the Society will allow members to draw against cheques paid into their accounts after a few days (as shown), this does not always mean that a cheque has cleared. Cheques later returned unpaid will be debited from the account.

which may in themselves be desirable or indeed desired ...
However, sometimes it is practicable, and again the example
of Japan in 1945 is particularly interesting because at that
time, the dominant Western power, the United States, was in
the perfect position to impose anything it wanted. Japanese
men, the men who had ruled Japan and led the country into
the war, were so demoralized by defeat that they were in no
position to oppose anything. So it was Western jurists who
stepped in, and in the case of women's rights, it was a young
Jewish, Japanese-educated European woman, who wrote into
the constitution the right of women to vote. The women in
Japan were all delighted.

*I'm sure they were! You said earlier that international organ-
isations and NGOs can at least make their views known. Do
you think that when Westerners see women and children
being treated in a manner they consider demeaning, shameful
or dangerous they should take more concrete steps? Distribute
leaflets? Incite to riot?*

There are certain practical things that can be done in some
cases. For example, when Western companies set up factories
in countries where dictatorships suppress or outlaw unions,
they can do their best maximize the rights of their workers.
In fact, it is in the interests of these Western companies to improve the lot of the people who work for them because they
– the companies – are much more vulnerable to shaming than
are domestic companies in the countries themselves. Companies such as Reebok, Nike, Volkswagen cannot afford to run
sweatshops in countries such as China, they know they
would be exposed by the press in Germany and in other
countries in the West. So they can set an example and perhaps
have some effect in the developing countries. That is at least
something. It's much harder for governments to do anything
practical, although at the very least, they should always give
support or encouragement to any individual or organisation

that takes steps to ameliorate poor conditions in developing countries. Unfortunately, this does not often happen – on the contrary. What actually happens is that cultural tradition is used as an argument against what is then described as neo-colonial criticism of these conditions. I can give you a very specific anecdotal example of this.

I was once asked to give a lecture at the Volkswagen Stiftung in Hanover. The motto was: "Weltbürger". The idea was that Volkswagen executives should learn about the rest of the world, become more cosmopolitan, learn to be sensitive to different ways of thinking in different countries, and not just be focussed on hard business. A laudable aim. And I thought that since Volkswagen had invested so heavily in China that China would be a good topic. So I put together a piece on why it is that for hundreds of years Westerners have been so willing to bow to political intimidation by various Chinese forms of government, including the present government. It's this chimera of enormous riches to be gained by doing business in China, the mystique of Chinese civilisation … anyway, I tried to analyze this. The title was going to be "Kowtowing to the Dragon Throne". Nothing but the title went to the Volkswagen-Stiftung … and one sentence came back: "China geht nicht." (Not China).

My proposed talk had obviously embarrassed the Volkswagen Stiftung, to the extent that some of their PR people came to London to talk to me because they wanted me to give another lecture. We had lunch, and then they started to explain that they were all in favour of cosmopolitism and so on, it was so interesting. However, when they visited China, they realized that things like individual rights and freedom of speech meant something quite different to the Chinese, that we should not be so Eurocentric and in the end, who are we to tell the Chinese how things should be done? In the course of the conversation, it became clear that they were setting themselves up as progressive, liberal-minded, tolerant people, and I ended up being the neo-colonial Colonel Blimp.

This fallacy makes it much harder to do anything to improve conditions for menial workers in countries that live under authoritarianism.

Are we talking about cultural values here, or simple greed?

To couch it in terms of cultural values would be a mistake, because if you say that individual rights, women's emancipation and the like are cultural values, then you're giving the upper hand to those people in non-Western countries who oppose them by claiming they are Western traditions that don't fit with theirs. Civil liberties, human rights are not cultural values. At the same time, I think that in many cases, we shouldn't be too absolute about them anyway. You have to look at local traditions and see why certain practices exist there, and you shouldn't categorically condemn prostitution, for example, because it's demeaning to women, or even child labor, because it's always abuse. Sometimes prostitution is a way for village girls to better themselves, better their families, get some of their siblings an education. Sometimes child labor – the income from children weaving carpets, for example – is the only source of family income. You are not helping the children by trying to deprive them of their work. I do think that slave labour should be opposed because it completely cuts out any possibility of individual choice ... But for the rest, it's a question of whether there is a minimum of choice involved. I don't think that a clash of civilisations comes in here at all.

A question about the conflict – I hesitate to call it cultural – over the death penalty within the Western world. The Germans are particularly opposed to it, consider it barbaric. Many Americans are in favour of it. Should we tolerate the death penalty?

Well, again, I think the word culture should be deleted from that discussion and it certainly has nothing to do with American culture – some states have it, others don't, and it disappeared altogether for some time. It has only come back recently for all kinds of populist reasons: people felt the crime rate was intolerably high, something had to be done, they were convinced this was the way to tackle the problem. In the case of Britain and probably quite a number of other Western countries, if you had a referendum, you might very well get a majority of people who were in favour of hanging. But a democracy is not the place for referenda. And the closer it gets to real democratic populism, the more likely you are to get things like the death penalty because people's instincts lie in that direction.

Are you saying that everybody likes a good hanging, a good lynching…

I think it makes them feel safer, it takes care of their desire for revenge although ideally, a democracy should guard itself against that. Still, although you can't completely ignore feelings of vengeance, that's not what justice should be primarily about. America is a much more populist democracy than Germany or Britain, so to oppose the death penalty by saying the Americans are not civilized is probably the wrong way of looking at it. And, of course, there are many Americans who oppose it.

The new technologies, the stem cell issue, cloning – where are the boundaries? How tolerant should we be?

You can't legislate everything. It's been a tendency in America, in particular, to try to: from personal relationships to abortion to all kinds of social practices that normally fall under the rubric "customs". The reason they legislate so much is that in a country of immigrants with vastly different cultural backgrounds, ethnic backgrounds, there aren't many customs that people have in common, so the law takes over. And of course, this can lead to absurd situations. There are many examples of where legislation on sexual relations has led to grotesque abuses, and where the latest faddish ideas on how relationships should be conducted have led to fantastic intolerance. De Toqueville already saw how a majority opinion can lead to intolerance, that it is something to be watch out for in a democracy. But in societies which are older and supposedly more homogenous, where custom and tradition are more important than the law, you get different problems. Take a country like Japan, where the Western idea of the rule of law is a relatively new one – there, the law existed mainly as a tool for those who governed the country to control the population, so you had a highly developed punitive law and criminal law. However, the notion that the law should be there to protect the individual from the power of the state – that was missing, that is a relatively new concept.

As far as personal relations are concerned, whereas in the United States a woman who feels she has been harassed or abused by her boss is likely to resort to legal action, in Japan, the traditional response would be, "Well, our culture is different, that is the way things are done here, women should not complain, they should put up with these things and show forbearance …". These days, however, it's becoming more common for women to initiate legal action.

So, although some people claim that older cultures with rich traditions and a long history are more civilized than immigrant cultures which legislate everything, this is not necessarily the case.

In conversation with Susan Stern.

Ian Buruma
Writer and journalist, Asia specialist. Fellow at the Woodrow Wilson Institute for the Humanities, Washington, D. C.

Born in 1951 in The Hague, Holland. Educated in Holland and Japan, spent many years living and travelling in Asia.

70   Long-time observer of cultural and ethnic identity issues and their conflict with modern technology. Writes extensively for *The New York Review of Books* and various other periodicals.

Selected publications: *God's Dust: A Modern Asian Journey* (1989); *A Japanese Mirror: Heroes and Villains of Japanese Culture* (1984); *The Wages of Guilt: Memories of War in Germany and Japan* (1994); *The Missionary and the Libertine* (1996).

PETER EIGEN

CORRUPTION: A GLOBAL SCANDAL

Most Europeans would reject any suggestion that corruption was "a part" of European culture, yet there is an impressive array of evidence that could be employed to support this charge. One need not point only to the political and 'big business' corruption scandals that have effectively destabilised Italy and Spain, and which more recently have surfaced in Germany and France. Fraud against the budget of the European Union has become a major problem, resulting in the Commission trying to establish networks of mutual legal assistance between member states to contain it, and increasingly instances are surfacing of bribes being paid to politicians and other public officials in public procurement and privatisations among European countries.

More recently, the European Commission of Jacques Santer resigned *en masse* over corruption. Yet, in the words of Vittorio Craxi, the corrupt methods of his father, the late Italian premier Bettino Craxi, and his German and French counterparts Helmut Kohl and Francois Mitterrand, were apparently justified by the greater goal of European unity:

Vittorio "Bobo" Craxi said that the "Three Patriarchs of Europe" accused of being united in their use of corruption to stay in power should be judged not by "petty" allegations of illegal political slush funds, but by their "huge achieve-ment" in building the foundations of a peaceful and stable continent towards the end of a century scarred by the "bloodshed and inhumanity" of fascism and communism. Signor Craxi said: "There is a huge difference between tak-ing money in exchange for favours and taking money for one's political movement, to build political stability".[1]

A NORTHERN MYTH

Corruption is everywhere – it is a global phenomenon. The issue can, indeed must, unite those of every political persua-sion who share a genuine concern for their societies. As with vice, so with virtue – no political grouping has a monopoly. A little tolerance goes a long way in all corners of the world, and it is a long road to stamp out the tolerance of graft. This is an issue that calls for a grand coalition of political, social and economic interests:

> *There is one particular "ideological difference" (that used to divide North and South) that needs much better appre-ciation – the myth in the North that a traditional culture of appreciation and hospitality fosters corrupt practices.*
> *I can speak only for Africa. But what holds true in my own continent may apply in other parts of the developing world. I shudder at how an integral part of my continent's culture can be taken as a basis for rationalising otherwise despicable behaviour. In the African concept of appreciation and hospitality, a gift is a token; it is not demanded; its value is in the spirit of the giving, not the material worth. The gift is made in the open for all to see, never in secret. Where a gift is excessive, it becomes an embarrassment, and is returned. If anything, corruption – as practised by ex-*

*porters from the North as well as by officials in the South –
has perverted positive aspects of this age-old tradition ...*

*Let us strip away excuses and explanations. In no so-
ciety – North, South or East – is it acceptable to the people
for their leaders to feather their own nest at public expense.
Once this simple truth is widely accepted, more meaningful
social and economic development will follow.[2]*

In the years since Olusegun Obasanjo spoke these words,
such a coalition has begun to take shape. He himself is
now president of Nigeria, elected on an anti-corruption
platform.

But it is important to address a deep-seated prejudice that
lingers, one which has become part of the folklore of capital-
ism in established business and government circles in Europe
and elsewhere in the North. It maintains that corruption is
considered morally wrong only in the North, while it is tolerated, or even considered desirable, in other parts of the
world, in particular in developing countries.

This theory of the cultural relativity of corruption is cou-
pled with the politically appealing argument that jobs have to
be created at any cost – even at the expense of one's neighbour. There are many striking examples of politicians, high
officials, business and opinion leaders in the North, who
publicly endorse this position. The now famous statement
in a BBC interview by Lord Young, Chairman of Cable &
Wireless and former British Minister for Trade and Industry,
well illustrates the widely held position that a little tolerance
is a good thing:

*The moral problem to me is simply jobs. Now when you're
talking about kickbacks, you're talking about something
that's illegal in this country [the United Kingdom] and, of
course, you wouldn't dream of doing ... but there are parts
of the world I've been to where we all know it happens.
And if you want to be in business, you have to do [it]. In*

many countries in the world, the only way in which money trickles down is from the head of the country who owns everything. Now that's not immoral, or corrupt. It is very different from our practice. We must be very careful not to insist that our practices are followed everywhere in the world.[3]

For proponents of this theory, it has for generations followed that firms from industrialised countries should, if they want to do business in the South, put their ethnocentric scruples aside: "When in Rome, do as the Romans do". Bribe politicians and civil servants, pay kickbacks, distort decision-making and economic management, undermine open market forces – in short, enter a competition of corruption.

Corruption has a long history, and its history crosses many cultures. Take the nepotism of the Ottoman empire:

Because the sultans no longer could control the "devsirme" by setting it against the Turkish notables, the "devsirme" gained control of the sultans and used the government for its own benefit rather than for the benefit of a sultan or his empire. In consequence, corruption and nepotism took hold at all levels of administration. In addition, with the challenge of the notables gone, the 'devsirme' class itself broke into countless factions and parties, each working for its own advantage by supporting the candidacy of a particular imperial prince and forming close alliances with corresponding palace factions led by the mothers, sisters, and wives of each prince. After Suleyman, therefore, accession and appointments to positions came less as the result of ability than as a consequence of the political manoeuvrings of the "devsirme"-harem political parties.[4]

Such tendencies are as alive as ever, but the passionate statement of General Obasanjo quoted earlier captures brilliantly the thrust of a growing consensus about the evils of corruption, particularly grand corruption in international business transactions, with its devastating impact on democracy and social development all over the world. His sentiment also finds expression in the campaign for an Anti-Bribery Convention which bore fruit in 1997, when 34 of the world's largest exporting countries agreed to ban corruption in international business transactions under the auspices of the OECD Convention on Combating Bribery of Foreign Public Officials in International Business Transactions (OECD Anti-Bribery Convention).

It is also expressed in the campaigning and *raison d'être* of Transparency International (TI), the movement committed to building a global coalition against corruption. The movement was initiated in the early 1990s by a group of concerned personalities from the developing and the developed world who were convinced that most of the benefits of economic development were being negated because of corruption. As a result of persistent corruption, the fragile hopes for development of the South were being dashed, and the transition economies of Eastern Europe were treading a treacherous path. The impact of corruption on economic development, democracy and the moral fibre of societies is devastating – and not limited to those in transition. Even strong and mature countries can be thrown into crisis, as recent political scandals in Germany, France and Japan testify. Corruption is tolerated both on the receiving and the giving end of the equation.

MYTH OR MYSTIFICATION?

Building a global coalition against corruption depends on an even-handed vision. Both sides are responsible, the giver and the taker. Action is needed in the North and the South, the West and the East. Co-operation cannot flourish on the basis of allocating blame or moral superiority.

The proponents of the moral acceptability of corruption in

the South, or the "culturalists", see widespread corruption in foreign societies often as an inherent part of traditional cultures that are based on strong loyalties to family and clan. They see such "clientelism" as essential for survival in the face of low civil service salaries and weak social welfare systems:

> *Those who have to struggle continuously for survival and live at the same time in a tradition, where loyalty to your relatives counts more than that to the state do not understand complaints of corruptibility.*[5]

This broad-brush characterisation obviates dramatic differences within the South, between, say, Botswana and Gabon, as much as differences within the North, between, say, Denmark and Italy[6], or different levels of tolerance in different sectors within one country, as in the case of the construction and other sectors in Germany for instance, or between different epochs in the same country.

Recognising the importance of local factors for dealing with corruption does not equate with suggesting that it is ethically acceptable in the South. It is true that many young states are particularly vulnerable to corruption. Administrative capacities are often weak, political structures unstable, individual and social commitments to modern norms and institutions are still fragile.

The colonial powers certainly did not leave a legacy of open government and accountability. In colonised countries, courts existed, but to sustain colonialism, not to make sure that justice prevailed or to enforce the rule of law. The judges were, in effect, civil servants. Likewise, the style of government was characterised by repression rather than consent, a system that was handed over intact to the incoming postcolonial administrations.

The legacy of communism – particularly in countries with little or no history of democratic rule – is equally inhospitable to honest government. In June 2000, the Russian tycoon Boris Berezovsky called for an amnesty on misdeeds relating to a chaotic and often corruption-tainted sell-off of state assets, saying the arrest of a Moscow media magnate showed that Russia needed a clean state to protect a post-Soviet division of property. "The solution", he said, "is an amnesty for initial capital. We need to finalise the story of what happened."[7]

Nor can the solution stop with the reform of governments. Take the chaebols of South Korea. Markets were too weak to curb the illegal financial deals of the chaebols, which are essentially family businesses lacking professional management at the head of the group, so government intervention was essential. "For government intervention to work, however, people must believe that the government is fair. If the government is feckless and corrupt, people lose trust in it, and intervention only exacerbates the market insecurities. The overriding concern then becomes the protection of existing property rather than adaptation to market changes, as it should be. Capitalists sometimes use their wealth to purchase protection from the government, which magnifies the problems of corruption."[8]

Yet there is rising anger at high-level corruption. Political campaigns are increasingly being driven by anti-corruption rhetoric the world over, suggesting at the very least a widespread intolerance of corruption among the electorates. In some countries, corrupt officials are jailed or even executed in significant numbers. Most opinion surveys in the South show that the vast majority of the populations consider corruption to be one of the most devastating problems they face. Individual campaigners and journalists repeatedly risk their lives in order to fight corruption.

And yet, despite the changing climate signalled by the OECD Anti-Bribery Convention, the myth of moral acceptance and tolerance of corruption abroad persists.

Nor has globalisation brought a level playing field and higher ethical standards. The conflicts in Angola and in the

Democratic Republic of Congo have been fuelled by a scramble for natural resources by politicians, generals and international companies. To make matters worse, international oil companies in Angola are not required to file annual tax records, so the famous "signature bonuses" paid out to secure oil blocks are not recorded. Instead of bringing global standards to bear throughout the world, the patchy progress of globalisation affords a haven for international players to exploit a situation without making them account for their actions.

It is comfortable to believe the myth about the moral acceptability of corruption abroad. Or is it sometimes self-deception? Or even blatant mercantilist propaganda? The distinction can be blurred. It still serves as a justification for many exporters to carry corruption systematically into the South.

Of course many Northern firms and governments do not attempt to justify foreign bribery by its acceptability in the South. They know it is forbidden, both morally and legally, but they also see that it is widely practised. They therefore decide that it is necessary to "howl with the wolves" if they want to do business abroad. Having done so, they do not want to make the first step to end bribery while the others, or some others, continue.

There can be absolutely no justification for bribing abroad, and particularly not in the South, which is especially vulnerable and can least afford mismanagement and waste. Different cultural practices clearly persist, but the "tribalism" of some African nations is often mirrored by not only chaebols, but also cronyism and nepotism in both the transition countries of the former communist bloc and, persistently, in Western Europe. In the context of Uganda, different tribes do put loyalty to each other above equality of access for others. According to Dr Mohammad Kisubi, "corruption is defined as including nepotism, tribalism and using your office for self-gain etc. But these definitions fall short when put to the test of my culture. If you close your eyes and ears to those in your clan and tribe, the cultural pressures will sooner rather than later bring you face to face with nepotism and tribalism."[9]

Political elites across the globe have failed to shed this "tribalism" and adopt a culture of serving the public, their electors. It is no wonder they are increasingly prompting the ire of publics who will no longer tolerate the abuse of power. In the words of Nobel Peace Prize winner Rigoberta Menchú Tum about her own country, Guatemala, "gaining office (whether by popular election or by appointment) is akin to political plunder: the position offers a blank cheque, and the guarantee of great personal enrichment. This is a rule tacitly accepted by all those who call themselves politicians."[10]

In Papua New Guinea, politicians have so consistently failed to resist bribes that a law was passed on 7 December 2000 to end the criss-crossing of the parliamentary floor by MPs:

Political parties have not yet developed to the point where they offer alternative platforms and policies to the voting public. Instead, individual candidates offer material benefits, such as food and drinks, and promises of future rewards, in return for votes from their constituencies... The majority of members of parliament, often elected with as little as ten per cent of the vote, are rarely re-elected. They tend to see their term in office as an opportunity to advance their personal fortune at the expense of the national interest.[11]

In Brazil, as recently as 2000 parliamentary deputies threw out a bill that would have outlawed nepotism in government and congress:

The proposed legislation aimed to curb the widespread practice among politicians of employing their relatives in well-paid positions. It would have prevented officials in any branch of government from hiring members of their family, through blood or marriage. But the proposal fell 22 votes short of the 308 it needed to pass – and 153 legislators voted openly against it. Inocencio de Oliveira, the veteran leader of the government-allied Liberal Front Party, called the idea an 'aberration'. An informal survey by Chamber leaders showed that about 60% of the 513 legislators employed relatives.

'Relatives are human and defenceless creatures, not these monsters they're made out to be,' deputy Gerson Peres said. Mr Peres, who has two family members working in his office, has proposed creating a quota system to limit the number of relatives a public official may employ.[12]

In Africa patronage has also been tolerated, or even seen as a virtue in traditional values:

There is much to excuse nepotism. Any man rising to a place of importance in politics will be surrounded by relatives and friends looking confidently to him for patronage, the traditions of centuries leave them in no doubt that he will provide for the needed patronage, and that if jobs do not exist they will be created. The politician may grasp the constitutional idea himself, but it is difficult for him to explain to his kinsmen that his political career will be threatened and jeopardised, and that to pay the price may cost him to lose his job. Consequently the life of ministers and other people of importance is made burdensome by nagging and increasing demands, as they find themselves entangled in the familiar net of family obligation. Of course governments all over the world, including Africa, have evolved and it is now globally accepted that nepotism is wrong.[13]

Today there is a growing consensus that corruption has to be reined in. This consensus includes concerned leaders from all continents, and it draws its support from all segments of society, from all sectors. It includes business, academia, NGOs and religious groups, media, political leaders and civil servants. The time is clearly ripe to forge effective coalitions for concrete actions against corruption, and much groundwork has already been prepared. In 1993, a Code of Ethics on International Business for Christians, Muslims and Jews[14] was developed. It was put forward that four key concepts recur in the literature of the faiths and form the basis of any human interaction. They are: justice (fairness), mutual respect (love and consideration), stewardship (trusteeship) and honesty (truthfulness).

All three faiths agree that justice must characterise the relationship between the inhabitants of the world. The second principle – mutual respect or love and consideration for others – is also inherent in the moral teachings of each religion. What the Scripture expresses as love is here rendered as mutual respect or reciprocal regard – "love thy neighbour as thyself" – existing between two individuals. The application of this has come to mean that self-interest has a place in the community only in as much as it takes into account the interests of others.

A third principle shared by all three faiths is that of stewardship (trusteeship) of God's creation and all that is in it – human beings are charged with its care and proper use for which they will have to give account. The fourth principle inherent to the value system of each of the three faiths is honesty. It incorporates the concepts of truthfulness and reliability and covers all aspects of relationships in human life – thought, word and deeds. It is more than just accuracy, it is an attitude which is well summed up in the word "integrity". In business dealings, "true scales, true weights, true measures" are to be used. Speaking the truth is a requirement for everyone.

The coalition against corruption spans continents, cultures and religions, social strata, and the professional orientations of its supporters. An important precondition that this common effort will succeed is the shedding of the myth of the moral acceptability of corruption in the South and an end to the tolerance of graft. It is the recognition that "in no society – North, South or East – is it acceptable to the people for their leaders to feather their own nest at public expense", as Obasanjo points out: "Once this simple truth is widely accepted, more meaningful social and economic development will follow." A little tolerance goes a long way – and, among the public at large, it has gone too far. Their tolerance is running out.

Notes

1 Michael Johnston, "The Political Consequences of Corruption: Reassessment", in: *Comparative Politics*, July 1986.

2 Olusegun Obasanjo, "Positive Tradition Perverted by Corruption", *Financial Times,* 14 October 1994.

3 Lord Young, in *BBC World Report,* 17 May 1994; for very similar positions by prominent German politicians, see: Antwort des Parlamentarischen Staatssekretärs Dr. Kurt Faltlhäuser, 16 January 1995; Presseverlautbarung No. 2515 der FDP-Bundestagsfraktion, Bonn, 24 June 1994; Minister Rexrodt, *ARD: Bericht aus Bonn,* 13 January 1995.

4 Encyclopaedia Britannica.

5 E. Werner Külling, "Krebsübel im Süden, mitgenährt vom Norden: Entwicklungs-Killer Korruption", *Helvetas Partnerschaft 138,* 1994, p. 8.

6 For a fascinating description of the cultural and historic factors affecting corruption in Italy, see Werner Raith, *Thesen zum Vortrag bei der Friedrich Ebert Stiftung,* 12 January 1995.

7 *Wall Street Journal,* 16–17 June 2000.

8 *Korea Herald,* 2 August 2000.

9 Dr. Mohammad Kisubi, contribution of 28 March 2000 to the Utstein internet discussion, "Approaches to Curbing Corruption".

10 "The plague of corruption: overcoming impunity and injustice" in *Global Corruption Report 2001* (2001), p. 155. See www.globalcorruptionreport.org

11 "New party law in Papua New Guinea" by Transparency International
Papua New Guinea in *Global Corruption Report 2001* (2001), p. 16. See
www.globalcorruptionreport.org

12 BBC World Service, 17 March 2000.

13 C. J. K. Tanda, University of Juba, Khartoum, Sudan, in *Nepotism and
the Evolution of the Public Service in Apia: A critical review.* Quoted in
*Report on the Investigation of Allegations of Nepotism in Government:
Report No. 11 (Special Report)* to the Parliament of South Africa by the
Public Prosecutor of the Republic of South Africa, 15 April 1999.

14 Simon Webley. *An Interfaith Declaration: A Code of Ethics on International Business for Christians, Muslims and Jews.* Amman, Jordan:
Arab Thought Forum, Al Albait Foundation, 1993.

Peter Eigen

Chairman of Transparency International (TI). Visiting Scholar
at the Carnegie Endowment for International Peace.

Born in 1938 in Augsburg, Germany. A lawyer by training.
Worked in economic development for 25 years, mainly as a
World Bank manager in Africa and Latin America. Founder
and present chairman of Transparency International, the internationally leading anti-corruption NGO. Teaches at the
Kennedy School of Government (Harvard), at Johns Hop-
kins University and is a Visiting Scholar at the Carnegie Endowment for International Peace.

Selected Publications: *The TI Source Book. National Integrity
Systems* (co-author, 3: 1999); *Korruption im internationalen
Geschäftsverkehr* (co-author, 2000); *The Global Corruption
Report 2001* (co-author, 2001).

FRIEDEMANN SCHULZ VON THUN

LET'S TALK

Ways Towards Mutual Understanding

A Conversation

You've shown me a chart on which tolerance is the oppo-site of indifference. What is tolerance for you if not indiffer-ence?

Imagine that you live with someone whose standards are dif-ferent from yours, who thinks, feels and acts differently. Per-haps you find his or her whole way of life "disturbing". Could you put up with this? Tolerance is the readiness and (inner) ability to put up with another person's different na-ture, although it might conflict with your own understanding of what a good and a proper way of life means. "Putting up with" is more than accepting something in a resigned, head-shaking way: it also includes the conviction that there are sev-eral roads that lead to Rome and that not everyone wants to go to Rome anyway. It is a sort of a meta-conviction: I can discern from my higher vantage point that my deeply-in-grained modus vivendi is not the only one that can make a person happy, and that there are other worthy lifestyles and philosophies. They are not the same as mine, but they don't have to be inferior just because of that.

Tolerance, according to such a "meta-conviction", means that I must have at least some convictions that would make me different from other people. Otherwise my "tolerance" would be pure indifference, which would make everything equally valid and arbitrary.

"Tolerance" is, indeed, an essential condition for successful co-existence – whether you are talking about sharing a flat or about the survival of humankind. But tolerance isn't the highest virtue in all situations, and it has to be balanced against other virtues. Some situations have to be courageously resisted and swiftly ended. Here is an example: while taking the tube, you see that someone is attacking, bothering or humiliating another person. In this case it is not "tolerance" but "civic courage" that is clearly called for. There are limits to what can be tolerated. Yet, I can hide my timidity, my Mr. Biedermann's fear of an arsonist, under the mask of "tolerance".

The question arises: when do tolerance and courageous intervention ("zero tolerance") become proper human reactions to a disturbing otherness?

It's easy to answer this question from behind your desk, but it's much harder to do so in real life. A hypothetical answer: the morality and enlightenment that characterise tolerance work best in situations where other people live in their own sweet way without bothering, threatening or restricting me or others in any fashion. Courageous intervention is necessary if the other person's lifestyle threatens, annoys or hems me or others in. But in everyday life we usually have to do with "mixed cases." If I live in a neighbourhood with a lot of lively people from the Mediterranean who throw loud and cheerful parties in the evening, then tolerance demands that I grant them their lifestyle without condemning them for the disturbance. Perhaps this liveliness could even teach me something, pull me a bit out of a conservative-bourgeois rut and stupor. At the same time, I am annoyed by noise and can't fall asleep. This is where it gets tricky: how do I find an attitude which combines both points of view, and how must I adjust my behaviour? How do I combine tolerance with self-assertion?

Communication psychology often has to deal with these issues: "What stops me from respecting and tolerating somebody who is different from me, but whose difference causes me no harm?" This thought can lead to some fascinating self-analysis, for example in family counselling, when parents are horrified by their children's development. Self-analysis can be very useful in preventing a person from letting his rage get the better of him and hurling himself at someone else's throat. Here are some examples of a self-analytical approach: "What prevents me from setting clear limits as to how far a person can go if his behaviour infringes on the rules of co-existence and clearly harms me?" or "How can I communicate to the other person what it is that disturbs me (or hampers, angers or hurts me) without condemning or demonising him?"

Communication is difficult, and misunderstandings are the rule rather than the exception – as you've quite rightly pointed out. But how would you structure communication so that it succeeds? What does it require from the participants?

Let's say I am with my girlfriend at a party, and I see that she is having great time and flirting with every man around. My tolerance is running out! I find her behaviour impossible, I feel left in the lurch and, as the evening turns into torture, my rage builds up. What now? Is this my problem, and do I have to cope with the fact that I am so sensitive, jealous and intolerant? Does this situation challenge my personal development? Or can I resolve the communicative challenge by simply blowing my top at the "floozy"? In my view, the best solution would be for me to have a good talk to her about the situation. I should come right out with what is bothering me and not try to bottle it up. Whatever doesn't come out remains inside and poisons the atmosphere. A rule of thumb: don't act more tolerantly than you feel inside.

I feel strongly about the emotions caused by what you do to me! This is feedback with a high degree of self-revelation.

When asked once about her recipes for successful communication, Ruth Cohn said: "If communication gets difficult,
simply say what your problem is". I agree with her – only it
isn't that simple!

Accusations, insults and complaints – these are what tend
to come out in the post-party conversation. "You know what
you are? A cheap whore!" Sending such a damning, demeaning message spares me from having to ask myself: what is
wrong with me? A fierce quarrel between friends certainly
isn't conducted the way communication manuals suggest, and
many a vehement charge may fly in both directions. But once
I get it "out", I should come back to the question: what
causes me to get so furious? The good Lord has given me not
just a quick tongue but also two ears. After I have got rid of
what's eating me, I will be curious to hear how the whole in-
cident looks from your point of view, namely, how you see
your behaviour at the party and your reaction to my touchi-
ness and reproaches? And I won't rest until I have understood at least 99% of your view on the matter!

We can re-connect and find reconciliation despite all our
differences and intolerance only if we understand that "in a
quarrel between two people, the truth lies somewhere in the
middle!" Except, of course, that all too often, no one is really
interested in the truth.

*Why is it so difficult for people to understand each other?
What hinders, what helps mutual understanding?*

It is easy to understand the other person and to achieve
mutual understanding if he/she thinks and feels as I do. It
gets difficult if "worlds lie between us", and the latter is
rather the rule than the exception, even when the parties
come from the same culture. Let us stay with the above
example. One of us thinks: "If we're going out, then it's
important for me to feel that the two of us are going out
together. I want us to experience each other as a couple and

88

to be able to demonstrate our common identity to others. Otherwise, I could go alone." The other person has a different view: "If we go out, then I would like to meet people and open myself to them, free and unencumbered – not under supervision. I enjoy our togetherness alone with you, but for that, I don't need other people."

If the other person's "world" disturbs or threatens me, arouses my resistance or questions my own "world", then I'm moved to retaliate – "Yes, but...!" – rather than trying to understand it. Particularly if I feel insecure, I don't want to let your world get too close to me, because it could either shake up the foundations of the truth that keeps me going or render that truth relative. And what can understanding bring us? It can supply the knowledge that there are always several possible approaches to any critical situation, and that each of them carries a grain of truth, so that the answer to the question "Who is right?" is not "Me or you?" but "You and me!" It is enormously reassuring for me to know in my heart that if **you** were right (at least subjectively, according to the laws valid in my world), this doesn't mean that **I** am wrong! It is this small reassurance that allows me to accept your view of things instead of immediately fending it off and/or derogating it.

"To understand" does not mean "to agree" Some people fear that if they try gently and lovingly to understand the other's point of view, they create the (false) impression that they are subscribing to the equation "to understand = to have sympathy for = to approve of." It is important to know that values and virtues can affect human co-existence constructively only if they are counterbalanced by opposite but related qualities. For example: tolerance without courageous confrontation degenerates into timid leniency; conversely, confrontation without tolerance grows into aggressive contempt.

If there is a confrontation between two people, and their tolerance is being sorely tested – let's stick to our party example – there is obviously a conflict of values: he goes for "to-

getherness", she prefers "openness and freedom", in this situation, anyway. Once I'm aware (not just intellectually but
also emotionally) that such values complement each other
and could contribute to a dynamic and lively relationship,
then the opponent becomes a complementary partner, and
our complementary partnership integrates the partial truths
each of us has brought into the relationship. The thing is, "togetherness" without freedom and openness to the outside can
deteriorate into a cramped symbiosis; freedom/openness
alone, without the feeling of togetherness, turns into disloyal
non-attachment. I'd present it as a "value square" (*Talking to
Each Other,* Part 2, 1989):

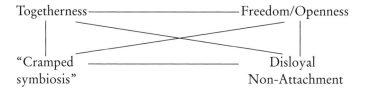

Togetherness ———————————————— Freedom/Openness

"Cramped ——————————————— Disloyal
symbiosis"   Non-Attachment

It's typical of human communication in conflict situations
that each side basks in the superiority of his/her own values
and dismisses the values of the other to the dungeons of dege-
neracy: "I stand for togetherness, and you persist in disloyal
non-attachment!" The other person says exactly the opposite:
"Oh no, I stand for openness and freedom, while you are
striving for a cramped symbiosis, where people exist only as
couples, no longer as individuals!"

*You once wrote that you were (and are) buoyed up by the
hope that psychologists could become "midwives of the internal reform of the state!" What could education do to equip
people with the skills they need to treat others in a tolerant,
fair way?*

Education could perhaps accomplish something, but only to
a certain degree: it has to make sure that tolerance and "the

fight of love" (Jaspers) are communicated to us not just as qualities necessary for successful co-existence, dressed up as some kind of school homework or a Sunday sermon and having little to do with actual life. No, we should treat them as arguments in a continuing dialogue about how to live and work together with others, as a cornerstone of an implicit (and sometimes explicit) curriculum for learning about life, and we should practice them daily. We have all read Nathan the Wise at least once, and what we learned there was wonderful! But what exists in your mind must also exist in your heart, and it has to be reinforced by a well-drilled communication repertoire. Basically, it's the old holistic concept of "head, heart and hand".

I know it's easy to recommend this but very difficult to put into practice. And, as far as I know, schools and teachers are far from being alone in supplying their pupils with values and behaviour patterns.

In this connection, teaching people "communication skills" should start long before nursery school age. We should often "listen actively" to a three-year-old; a four-year-old can already develop a clear concept of what a "compromise" is. The change of perspective, the ability to put oneself in the other's shoes, is already present in nursery school children.

If the parents communicate to the child: "You are important, we respect your feelings, your opinion counts – and we are also important and deserve to be taken seriously. Let's talk about how we can come to an understanding, let's do it with love and patience, strength and certainty, humour and seriousness, quarrels and reconciliations," – such an atmosphere is the best basic education program for teaching "communication skills."

I am very much in favour of schools for parents. Parents hold one of the key social positions and play a challenging "leadership role." And, because of that, they can reach – regularly or occasionally – their limits. Modern communication training goes beyond giving instruction or advice and focuses on helping people develop self-supervisory and self-counselling abilities. Such skills can help parents rear their children and become more mature in the process.

The same applies to teachers, for, these days more than ever, they have to be "experts on interpersonal relations", which means they have to master the skills of conducting a conversation, moderating a discussion or settling a conflict, and working with parents. Such training aims for a successful integration of the teacher's professional with his/her interpersonal skills. I've seen promising developments in this direction lately. For instance, in the last phase of their training, student teachers in Hamburg receive obligatory practice-orientated counselling based on principles of communication psychology.

Our present educational system is, as a rule, more geared to transmitting knowledge than to teaching skills and developing abilities in students. Yet, the ever-accelerating pace of change in daily life is challenging our abilities to live among people of different cultures, religions, views on life and lifestyles, so that the ability to live in peaceful co-existence is gaining in importance. What kind of contribution could communication skills make here? Is communication psychology the science of the future?

You're speaking like someone who is optimistic about the potential of education; I only wish I were too! Sure, education could and should be the science of the future. But we have to be modest in our expectations, since there are counter-forces that are much more powerful than education and special training. Education often appears on the scene in the role of David after Goliath has already done his dirty work in shaping people's personalities.

Let's take, for instance, a gang of young right-wing radicals who are looking for a fight. They have grown up without self-respect or any great prospects. They are like lost souls searching for a positive identity. Since they cannot find it on their own, they choose to be members of a group which boosts their self-esteem by disassociating itself from other, allegedly inferior "elements". Here we have the old, time-proven and unfortunate division of people into "US" and "THEM". The latter are the wretched, hateful "subhuman creatures" over whom WE – brilliant and strong (and aggressive) – can triumph, no matter whether they are foreigners, followers of a different faith, the homeless or the Jews. Here the identity formula is: "Hate makes a man!"

The roots of intolerance and the mentality behind every crusade lie in uncertainty and in feelings of inferiority. The latter are magnified by a complex fabric of overlapping social, economic, political and spiritual factors. Education and special training make virtually no impact on them.

The more complex and dynamic our world becomes, the greater the danger of relapsing into ways of thinking that appear simple and promise safety. They could take the form of nationalism, esoteric energies or religious fanaticism. One possible conclusion could be that it is necessary to resist the tendency to oversimplify everything, and that we should come up with a concept that would allow for diversity and democratic development in our world.

Here I would suggest a model which focuses on "internal plurality": everyone is a pluralistic society! This "internal team" model (*Talking to Each Other*, Part 3, 1998) assumes that not two but many "souls live in our breasts", that they make themselves heard under specific circumstances and attempt to reveal themselves and thus affect a person's behaviour. On the one hand, such internal plurality produces unpleasant complications, since internal voices usually disagree with each other – so the individual is not "at peace with himself" and not at peace with others. Such disagreement can escalate into an internal civil war while the personality grapples internally with the issue of tolerance: many a member (of such an internal team) may be rejected by the "boss" and become an outsider. Then such outsiders might move underground to start a terrorist conspiracy. In short: before we can enjoy having an "internal team", we have to cope first with a "disunited bunch" within us.

However, if a person succeeds in building such an internal team – and this is something a person can learn – then internal opposition turns into complementary partnership, and the promise inherent in this model will be realised. Only then can we deal with life "with our combined strengths": externally efficient and strong and internally harmonious.

Whoever succeeds in turning a problematic internal diversity into a source of virtuous synergy will also certainly acquire the courage to see that the external plurality of mankind is more than just a difficult task: it is also a promise.

In conversation with Thomas R. Henschel.

Friedemann Schulz von Thun
Psychologist.

Born in 1944 in Soltau, Germany. Lecturer in psychology at the University of Hamburg, specialist in counselling and training. Head of "The Working Group on Communication and Clarification". Developed new concepts in professional education, bringing together research, learning and practice.

Selected publications: *Miteinander reden 1–3* (1998); *Sich verständlich ausdrücken* (co-author, 6: 1999); *Klärungshilfe. Handbuch für Therapeuten, Gesprächshelfer und Moderatoren in schwierigen Gesprächen* (co-author, 2000).

DJ WestBam

Music Makes for Racists

A Conversation

DJ WestBam, a.k.a. Maximilian Lenz, fills the room with energy. The words pour out of him and I have the impression that sitting semi-still for an interview requires an effort – he would prefer to pace. But since I have only an old-fashioned recorder which has to be placed on the table between us, he is confined to his chair.

Techno is his music, Berlin is his turf, although he travels all over the world much of the time. At 36, he readily admits to being older than most of his fans, since Techno is appreciated most by the really young – teens, and what the Germans call twens. It's physically strenuous music, he explains, very loud, all-night dance music, and the older you get, the harder it is to keep up. But he's not planning to retire any time in the foreseeable future, and his fans (who now occasionally call him "Sie", the formal address reserved for older generations) want him to keep going.

Tolerance is our topic. WestBam is convinced that tolerance is foreign to our basic nature. We have these basic instincts, he explained, and they are anything but tolerant. We come into the world with deep, gut fears which we needed in our primordial state to keep us alive. We fear the unknown, we fear the unfamiliar, and we are hostile to whatever we fear. Intolerant in the extreme. But these days in so-called civilised society, many of our fears are unfounded and certainly not necessary for our survival. We don't need to fear everything that's different just because it's different, we don't have to deride it or fight against it, we can learn to be tolerant. That's where culture comes in. It's the task of our learned culture to conquer our basic instincts by making us aware how unhealthy and destructive they can be.

What does music do for tolerance? Conventional wisdom, says WestBam, has it that music brings people together. Well, it does, of course. Music recognises no human differences, it appeals to people regardless of their colour, faith or political convictions. On the other hand, WestBam was quick to point out that music creates as well as overcomes intolerance. You may get a bunch of really diverse people together in a club, on a dance floor, in the streets (as in the case of the Berlin Love Parade, a now annual music which WestBam was partly instrumental in creating). But pretty soon, these people become united in their contempt for the fans of other types of music – Hip Hop or Rock'n' Roll, for example. Tolerance goes out the window. Not that these competing fans are likely to become violent these days – Techno fans may be contemptuous of other forms of music, but they don't fight to defend their dogma. In the old days, when WestBam himself was a Rock'n' Roll punk (in the early 1980s), things sometimes got out of hand. But still – music racism can't be denied, it exists, and it's not always nice.

Well, can't a DJ such as yourself do something to bring these different fans together, get them at the very least to respect each other (taste, as we know, not being open to discussion), I wonder. "Yes and no," says WestBam. Certainly, a DJ should do his best to unite the different music fronts and create a form of music universality. Together with Africa Bambaataa, king of Hip Hop, WestBam did make an effort. But the fans: "well, the fans come to hear the music they want to hear, and in the end, they don't want their favourite DJ to play much of anything else. A pretty intolerant lot, but what can you do? It really takes courage to produce a universal mix!" – I think I detected a rueful note there.

Then I pop a question I have always wanted to ask but have always been afraid to (for fear of being dismissed as what the Germans call a *Grufti* – somebody old and grey and really not with it): what kind of communication can take place in a jam-packed space with psychedelic lighting which makes you dizzy, and where the noise is literally deafening (causing hearing impairment for hours, if not for days) and where nobody dances with anybody else, but just jiggles up and down to the extent that jiggling is possible? WestBam takes the question in his stride – no doubt he has heard it before. The Techno dancers are not dancing alone, they are dancing with everyone else in the room. The music is the message. Communication is simply non-verbal, but it's definitely taking place. What about drugs? What role do they play? WestBam agrees that drugs, while not de rigeur, are certainly an integral part of the scene. They heighten the senses and thereby intensify the music and the whole psychedelic effect. And here again, we're dealing with natural intolerance, fear of the unknown, says WestBam. Drugs are a taboo in our society, there are all kinds of myths associated with them, the dangers are vastly exaggerated. But this has always been the case (and on this point I have to agree, it was no different in the 1960s when my whole generation were high on pot and our parents feared the worst). So, continues WestBam, it's the same old generational story. We all need to overcome our inborn intolerance, fear of what we don't know or understand.

We talk a bit about the Love Parade, a Techno happening which over the past few years has lost a lot of its spontaneity – WestBam points out that at first, it was a dancing-in-the-streets parade where many of the participants were casual bystanders who decided to join in for a few hundred meters. These days, it's a huge New Millennium Woodstock associated with provocative (often body-painted) nudity, outrageous clothes, and a certain lewd abandon which some find offensive. WestBam clearly disapproves of this development. He complains that the media are responsible for the unnecessary displays of body parts – one TV station apparently goes around with a big sign saying, "Show Your Boobs!" And of course, he says, everyone wants to get on TV. He grins wryly and adds: That's the sort of bad stuff we have to tolerate – and by tolerate, I mean put up with, not respect.

WestBam is German and his music was not born in Europe, nor in the U.S. That makes absolutely no difference, he claims, it's music that the world loves, and wherever I go, Japan, L.A., Holland, young people flock to hear it. It doesn't matter where it originated. But at the same time, he admitts that when he travels with his music, he does feel a bit like a German cultural ambassador. Let's face it, the Germans aren't the most popular people in the world, he says, and it's good to be German and have the feeling that you're contributing to international understanding.

His contribution is more than just the feeling. In 1988 he was sent by the Goethe Institute to represent German culture at the Olympic Summer Games in Seoul, and he's been awarded prestigious culture prizes since. Keep up that energy level, DJ WestBam!   *In conversation with Susan Stern.*

DJ WestBam

Disc jockey, producer and writer. Organiser of the world's largest indoor Techno-Event "Mayday". Co-founder of the Berlin Love Parade. Concert tours worldwide.

Born in 1965 as Maximilian Lenz in Münster, Germany. Currently Germany's most successful DJ, owner of the Berlin-based dance label Low Spirit. Co-authored with DJ Dr. Motte the official anthems of the *Love Parade* in Berlin in 1997, 1998 and 2000. His single "Sonic Empire" was awarded a platinum disc in 1997.

Publications: *Mixes, Cuts & Scratches* (1997) – the story of his art, work and life as a DJ.

JEFFREY ABRAMSON

IDEALS OF DEMOCRATIC JUSTICE

Let me begin by contrasting two related but distinct ideals of democratic justice. The first is the familiar principle of tolerance and the agreement of persons to agree to disagree. The second is the ideal of respect, an ideal that envisions a community held together by members' genuine appreciation of what they find to admire in one another. In this essay, I will argue for supplementing the distant, legal position of tolerance with the more intimate, psychological ties of respect.

Tolerance of diversity (diversity of peoples as well as of ideas) is the great achievement of liberal societies and I would not for a moment suggest any retreat from the inclusive and nondiscriminatory laws that put tolerance into practice. But when the law merely constrains human behavior without changing it, then the potential for backlash is always present, especially in difficult times. This is why I will argue that liberal societies ought to ask more of their citizens than merely to accommodate or not discriminate against others. Liberalism ought to build on the habits of nondiscrimination to foster in citizens an appreciation of the contribution diversity makes to democracy.

The limits of tolerance are both practical and philosophical. Practically speaking, hard cases arise (hate speech is an example) where tolerance may undermine rather than underwrite the equal treatment of persons essential to democracy. The absoluteness with which the principle of tolerance is often expressed leaves persons without practical guidance about where, if at all, to draw the line when it comes to tolerating the intolerant. Philosophically speaking, tolerance forms a weak social bond. While there is much to be said for resisting the community's hold on individuals, tolerance at times leaves individuals too isolated from one another. It is the ethic of strangers, a way of keeping the peace among persons who remain indifferent to and largely ignorant of cultures beyond their own. Tolerance teaches us the negative (do not discriminate against others). Respect teaches us the positive (embrace others as a way of enriching our own lives). Both are necessary.

THE TOLERANCE PRINCIPLE

Tolerance takes as its starting point what Machiavelli long ago diagnosed as the distinct condition of modernity: the arrival of "masterless men" (and women) freeing themselves from tradition, migrating within and sometimes between borders, forever pulling up anchor and moving on. In contemporary liberal societies, the mobility of individuals gives rise to a familiar pluralism or diversity of population. Citizens are largely strangers to one another, hailing from different backgrounds, professing diverse values, attending separate houses of worship, focusing on private interests. Given the heterogeneity of interests and peoples, any strong sense of community or a common good seems neither possible nor desirable.

The question arises as to what could form the basis of a stable social union in liberal democracies? What values could citizens separated by religion, national origin, culture, sometimes even language agree upon? Belief in the inclusive spirit of tolerance is one answer to this question. Tolerant persons do not necessarily come to like one another, to respect one another's traditions, or even to know much about them. They simply agree to disagree, each unsure about where the ultimate truth lies and therefore willing to accept the right of all persons to their own views.

While tolerance is often based on skepticism about the very existence of "truth", it does not demand such cynicism. It would be enough to follow John Stuart Mill's advice that even if truth exists, we should not trust governments to find it. Mill thought that tolerance of a wide array of views actually contributes to the emergence of truth through a process of trial and error, through competition in the marketplace of ideas that strengthens the truth by teaching persons the active spirit of inquiry necessary to discover it. John Locke framed another classic argument in favor of religious tolerance: coercion may force a person to conform outwardly but it will never bring true faith or conviction.

When people share the same values, they do not need to practice the restraints of tolerance. But when we confront groups or ideas we hate, then tolerance is put to the test. Privately, one may despise skinheads, white supremacists, the Ku Klux Klan, neo-Nazis and other hate groups. And yet legally one is required to grant space on the public stage to these groups. The strange paradox of tolerance is that it obliges us to tolerate those who would not tolerate us in return. Without necessarily respecting a particular people or a particular ideology, citizens of liberal societies accept that all groups have equal rights to express their views publicly.

Historically, tolerance has worked effectively to keep the peace and to end the religious warfare present throughout the early modern history of European and American states. But can tolerance deliver more than peacekeeping? Can it make of the state more than a truce-keeping force between rival interests and peoples? Many endorse tolerance precisely because it minimizes the power of community over individuals. Recently, however, philosophers on both sides of the Atlantic have praised tolerance's contribution to national identity. Addressing the question of what it is that Germans can and should share, Jürgen Habermas answers that it is precisely tolerance of "the integrity of each individual, in his or her otherness" that brings Germans together into a common good. The American philosopher John Rawls makes a similar point about the connection between community and tolerance in the United States. In a democracy, people voluntarily join countless different associations, some based on religion, others on work, still others on recreational interests. The national state does not aspire to replace this plurality of social unions so much as it seeks to provide constitutional structures of tolerance that let this diversity prosper. In this sense, concludes Rawls, the tolerant state is "the social union of social unions."

THE IDEAL OF RESPECT

Contrast the doctrine of tolerance with the alternative ethic I earlier called "respect". Respect goes beyond tolerance by prodding us not just to live with diversity, not just to "put up with it", but to find a positive value in living together with persons from different walks of life. Respect comes when we affirm the worth of traditions and identities other than our own. But so long as citizens remain strangers, they rarely discover what might be of value in their neighbor's religion or their co-worker's ethnic identity. Respect therefore argues for a curriculum of civic education in democratic societies, a course of education sufficient to replace the distant, indifferent feeling of mere tolerance with a more intimate, knowledgeable and sincere appreciation of other traditions. In the United States, constitutional doctrines of separation of church and state deter public schools from teaching anything "religious". This is certainly a safe course, far preferable to a public education that puts the power of the state behind one particular religion's tenets. But the ethic of respect suggests that democratic education needs to do a better job of teaching children about what is different but important in their classmates' lives outside school.

Of course, learning about others is no guarantee that we will admire what we learn. I can find nothing to admire about fundamentalist doctrines of any religion that justify treating women as inferior. I can find nothing to appreciate about groups that preach racial and religious hatred or advocate terrorism. The more I learn about such groups, the more firmly I might conclude that tolerating their doctrines makes no contribution to democratic debate, that in fact they threaten the preconditions of treating persons with equal dignity and mutual respect upon which democratic dialogue depends. In these circumstances, the doctrine of respect will generate different political conclusions than will the doctrine of tolerance. Tolerant people put up with even antidemocratic, antitolerant doctrines; they accept the risk that people will be converted by these doctrines in ways that misuse and even threaten the survival of tolerance. Respect abandons impartiality in favor of making substantive moral judgments about the content of a political or religious doctrine.

The German Constitution or Basic Law arguably alludes to the notion of respect when Article I (1) makes it the "duty of all state authority" to "respect and protect... the dignity of man". Such language implies that government must do more than end discrimination against individuals; it must take affirmative or positive steps to ensure that the personal dignity of each individual is protected against assaults from others. Consider, for instance, laws banning groups or parties that advocate race hatred. In the United States, the Supreme Court has consistently invalidated laws against hate speech, on the theory that the core principle of democracy is freedom to espouse any political idea, including hateful ideas. So long as the speaker stops short of inciting imminent violence, even hate speech must be tolerated. German case law is mostly similar but at times courts have suggested a different interpretation. As important as the rights of free speech are, they are not absolute but need to be balanced against the rights of persons to live as equals in society, free from defamation and harassment on the basis of race, religion, sex, or national origin. German law is particularly sensitive to this point because of the Holocaust but other nations, including England and Israel, consider hate speech as beyond the protection of the law. Take the case of the Roma minority in Hungary or elsewhere. What kind of dignity or equality can their children enjoy if they walk along streets and through parks plastered with signs slandering them with the worst things that could be said of human beings? How can these children develop a sense of self-respect if the government does not provide them with social respect? Democracies cherish freedom of speech because that freedom gives an equal voice to all persons. But people can hardly be said to have an equal voice when hate speech primes others to see them as racial and ethnic inferiors. The preaching of racial hatred is so destructive of the civility of conversation that it loses any claim to democratic tolerance.

Of course, giving governments the power to make judgments about parties and their ideologies is a risky business. One of the strongest arguments for tolerance is contained in the famous metaphor of a "slippery slope": once we give government the right to exclude any doctrine, we risk expansion and misuse of that power against opponents for purely partisan reasons. Far safer, then, to tolerate it all. But is it safer? On the one hand, there are risks involved in tolerating hate groups; on the other hand, suppressing them invites other risks. The ethic of respect recognizes that the risks of suppression almost always outweigh the risks of tolerance. But it allows for the possibility that some groups are purposely trying to foment hatreds leading to violence and that therefore democracies should run the risk of climbing even slippery slopes.

Gay and lesbian marriage is another topic that demonstrates the difference between tolerance and respect. It is one thing for society to tolerate what gays do in private; it is another to publicly recognize their partnerships as the equal of heterosexual relations. Many people who would not discriminate against gays nonetheless draw the line here and argue that society does not have to affirmatively endorse the bond between gay couples, as it would were the law to permit gay marriage.

What is the best response to such an argument? Gay rights groups usually base their arguments on the constitutional guarantees of equal protection in law to argue that the prohibition of gay marriages *is* blatant legal discrimination. To those worried that legal permission to marry is the same as moral acceptance of gay lifestyles, the gay community assures its opponents that such is not the case. The only message of such a law would be a neutral one, namely, that persons should be free to choose their own marriage partners free from state-imposed orthodoxies.

Although this argument about tolerance for gay and lesbian marriage is a strong one, it has not yet proven politically persuasive in most American states. I want to suggest one reason for this failure. The debate hinges on what the purposes of marriage are or ought to be. To the extent that the purpose of marriage is natural procreation, perhaps there might be some warrant for discriminating between gays and straights. But what about heterosexual couples unable to conceive, uninterested in having children, preferring adoption or trying in vitro fertilization? No state denies marriage licenses to such persons. When it comes to heterosexuals, the law fully recognizes that the institution of marriage gives public recognition to a couple's love, not its procreative capacity.

If this is so, the question is whether gays marry for love in the same way as heterosexual couples do? Political arguments based on tolerance seek to avoid this question, to put it in brackets and say that the state need not get into questions like this, that it should simply let people make their own choices about love and marriage. Political arguments based on the ethic of respect take a different tack. They seek to justify gay marriage by educating the majority heterosexual community about gay love and by educating them, to change political attitudes on the basis of showing respect for the sincerity of love in the gay community. Perhaps this overstates the educational mission. Perhaps the goal is more modestly that of persuading everyone to see that gays and heterosexuals marry for many different reasons, from love to money to having children. The very sameness of the motives is what the law should respect and recognize.

THE NEUTRALITY PRINCIPLE

One of the attractions of tolerance is that it seems such a neutral and impartial principle. Tolerance strips government of jurisdiction over individual life choices, so long as those choices threaten no harm to others. Instead of delivering an official judgment about the worth of a group or its ideas, the tolerant government simply frees persons "to choose their own good in their own way," in the famous phrase of John Stuart Mill.

But is tolerance truly neutral? Consider again Mill's dictum that the state is neutral because it places top value on freeing persons to choose their own good in their own way. But why should we accept that freedom of choice has this sovereign value, that living life as a questioning individual is such a good way to live, better for instance than a life lived in loyalty to inherited traditions and customs? Clearly, Mill's statement of tolerance rests on an unspoken preference for the "voluntarist" lifestyle of the dissenter over the involuntary lifestyle of the devout. This does not make Mill's argument necessarily wrong: perhaps democracy does depend on the habits of mind instilled in a person by exercising personal freedom of choice. But it does mean that the doctrine of tolerance itself rests on implicit moral assumptions about which lifestyles are most worthy of respect.

American law on abortion is often cited as an example of the moral neutrality achieved by tolerance but this seems doubtful. In *Roe v. Wade,* the U.S. Supreme Court stated that it would not take a position on the controversial question of when life begins, that it would simply agree to let Americans disagree. But precisely because Americans are divided on the ultimate moral questions surrounding abortion, the Court argued that law should be neutral and permit women to make the decision themselves as to whether to abort or carry a fetus to term. By making "pro-choice" the law of the land, the Court concluded, government itself was an impartial by-stander, giving equal legal protection to the different choices different women would make.

Even for those (like myself) who agree with this decision, it hardly seems neutral. Legalizing abortion clearly accommo-dates the views of those who think abortion is a morally ac-ceptable choice. But it does not at all accommodate the views of those who believe abortion is actually murder because life begins at conception. The Supreme Court was wrong to claim it could resolve the legal dispute over abortion without taking sides on the moral dispute over whether the fetus is a person. To tolerate lawful abortion is to reject the views of those who think there is no moral difference between infanticide and abortion. It is to side with those who argue that the freedom of women to control their own bodies is the guiding principle which must be respected in this area.

What is true about the abortion case is true of many diffi-cult legal controversies: practicing tolerance does not let us avoid taking a position on underlying moral disputes. Neu-trality is simply impossible and decisions require courts to make a substantive, moral argument in favor of one set of val-ues or the other.

Tolerance and respect each contribute to the equality of persons without regard to race, religion, or national origin. Tolerance is more modest in what it demands of citizens, asking us simply to accommodate other persons and views, regardless of what we think of them. Beyond accommodation, respect ties peoples together in a mutual appreciation of their differences.

After September 11, the need to combine tolerance and respect is more urgent than ever. The terrorists who attacked the World Trade Center and the Pentagon fit a definite ethnic (Middle Eastern) and religious (Muslim) profile. Not only the United States but all its allies have good reason to fear that more terror from Middle Eastern sources is imminent and ongoing (it may be that domestic terrorist groups are operating as well, but this does not lessen the danger of attacks from the Al Quaida network.). When a danger of such grave proportions is so clear and present and tied to a particular ethnic minority, the majority population may be tempted to think it necessary in the fight against terrorism to encroach on the civil liberties of any and all who share their ethnicity with the terrorists. Of course, this claim has a hollow ring to it when restrictions on civil liberties are the first resort proposed, rather than the last. Already the U.S. Congress has passed laws making it easier to detain and to search immigrants suspected of ties to terrorist organizations, with ambiguous definitions of what constitutes a "terrorist" entity. Some law enforcement agencies suggest that a state of emergency justifies the random stopping of any person who looks Middle Eastern or has a Middle Eastern-sounding surname.

Would it be safer to target all Muslims and Middle Eastern persons for special surveillance? Perhaps, although scapegoating Muslims at home might well prove counterproductive to U.S. efforts to enlist Muslim regimes abroad in the fight against terrorism. But let us suppose that protection of equal civil liberties for all is risky, more dangerous than at least residents in the United States were aware of before September 11. The real issue is whether citizens of liberal democracies find the maintenance of open and diverse societies worth the risk.

Here is where the psychology of respect becomes crucial. The more the majority sees a potential terrorist in every Middle Eastern face, the greater the risks they will see in civil liberties for the suspect population. Of course, the majority population knows better. They know that Muslims worked and died alongside non-Muslims in the World Trade Center. They know that few Muslims are terrorists, forming no greater a percentage of the Muslim population than IRA terrorists of the Catholic population. But although they know all these truths abstractly, the majority knows little about the actual doctrines of Islam, and still less about how their Muslim fellow citizens actually practice their religion. This ignorance did not jeopardize tolerance in the good old days before September 11, but it puts tolerance on shaky psychological ground today.

In the immediate weeks after the attacks, President Bush commendably attended a prayer service at a Washington, D. C. mosque. The president also invited an Islamic minister to participate in a national prayer service alongside Christian and Jewish clergy. Perhaps President Bush took these steps for expedient or political reasons, as a demonstration to the world. Still, how often had a president gone to a domestic mosque before? At a time when some were holding the Islamic religion responsible for the making of terrorists (this would be like blaming Christianity for the Ku Klux Klan), paying public respect to a minority religion was the right thing for the president to do.

Tolerant people do not ever have to enter one another's houses of worship, schools, parks or homes. But the accommodations of separate cultures that hold in good times are strained during crises. Democratic diversity finds a firmer footing when citizens cross over to other sections of town, daring to learn and appreciate firsthand the "otherness" of others. It is this transition from tolerance to respect that the events of September 11 force upon liberal societies, with still uncertain results.

Jeffrey Abramson
Professor of Law and Politics at Brandeis University.

Born in 1947 in Philadelphia. Ph.D. in Political Theory, J. D., Harvard. Clerked for the Chief Justice of the California Supreme Court and served as Special Assistant to the Attorney General, Massachusetts. Frequent contributor to the op-ed page of the New York Times and other national media.

Selected publications: *Liberation and Its Limits: The Moral and Political Theory of Freud* (1984); *The Electronic Commonwealth: The Impact of New Media Technologies on Democratic Values* (1987); *We, the Jury: The Jury System and the Ideal of Democracy* (2:2000).

WOLE SOYINKA

THE TEACHINGS OF THE ORISA

The United Nations has a most laudable tradition of desig-
nating every year, sometimes even the decade, a Year (or
Decade) of some specific global concern, indicating that there
is an area of concern for which that organisation desires to
mobilise the concerted efforts of all nations, voluntary agencies and individual opinion moulders. The overall purpose is
to bring about increased harmony among nations and peoples, or instigate a general amelioration of the human condition. Thus, we have had the Year of the Child, the Year of
Shelter, the Year of Minority or Indigenous Peoples, the Year
of Tolerance, Dialogue of Civilisations etc. etc. All these
specificities focus, quite rightly, on different aspects of humanity.

Left to me, however – were anyone sufficiently reckless
as to make me secretary-general of the United Nations – I
would have ensured that the year 2000 or 2001 was declared
the Year of the Secular Deities. A blasphemous oxymoron?
Not in the least, as we shall come to understand. Let me simply state for now that I do not exaggerate when I say that the
world has great need of the promotion of the secular gods,
partly to reinforce those other years of global concerns – the
Year of the Child, the Year against Torture, the Year of the

Woman etc. but – most crucial of all – the *Year of Tolerance.*
The adoption of the Judeo-Christian calendar in this respect
already has its problem of course, but the world appears resolved to live with that – in itself a most commendable act of
tolerance! In any case, I join others in accepting that any
phase of human history, and even a mere calendar notation,
deserves to be seized upon and made to serve even those peoples whose *mores* and cultures maintain their suspicious distance from the genesis, history and cultural claims of whatever part of the world is in celebration. As one who, as a
child, was raised in a *Christian* family – never mind that I
have long abandoned that faith – I still recall the great excite-
ment of anticipating, then celebrating the *Ramadan* with our
Moslem neighbours while they in turn joined in the festivities
of the Christians, be it Easter or Christmas. Something
dispiriting has happened in the past half century, however.
Divisions, sometimes murderous divisions, have sprung up
within such a natural community of faiths since those colonial and immediate post-colonial times.

Those of us who hold on to a belief in the unity, indeed the
indivisibility, of the human community, no matter how buf-
feted such a concept has been during the last century, especially by the anti-human excesses of ideology, religion, and
doctrines of separatism such as racism, social Darwinism or
apartheid, must consider ourselves fortunate if we happen to
be heirs to certain systems of beliefs that have survived those
overweening themes, themes that appear to have successfully
divided up, or still contest the world among themselves. We
can treat them all within a framework of binaries, sometimes
intersecting, and often self-replacing: communism and capitalism, Buddhism and Hinduism, Judaism and Christianity,
Christianity and Islam, Roman Catholicism and Protestantism, the Crusade and the Jihad, fascism and democracy,
the Judeo-Christian/Euramerican world and the Arab-Is-
lamic etc. etc. plus all their extended families, aggressive off-
shoots and client relations. All these, to varying degrees, and

112

despite their demonstrable and glaring errors of doctrine and conduct that prove so costly to humanity itself and disorganise swathes of living communities, continue to arrogate to themselves the monopoly of truth, perfection and/or dominance. This mentality of binary organisation makes it easy, on the one hand, to simplify "the Other", demonise it and focus on it as the sole obstacle to one's own survival. On the other hand, they do tacitly – and tactically – acknowledge it as an equal contender for the stakes of hegemonic dominance. Tough luck on the other inhabitants of the *real* world – which happens to be a pluralistic one! They simply disappear through a mere wave of the hand or aversion of the eyes by the Super-Duo, who thus conserve their energy for the final onslaught between only two monoliths.

As the African proverb goes, however, when two elephants fight, it is the grass beneath their feet that suffers. In fact, the grass simply vanishes! Ralph Ellison captured the predicament of the black man in the United States in his acclaimed classic *The Invisible Man,* providing the world with a bitter portrayal of the plight of millions of humanity who were rendered invisible by the arrogance of race within their own nation. I believe that it is time to draw attention to The Invisible Faiths, especially those instructive faiths of the "secular" – that is, humanistic – temper, and to highlight the many subtle tactics that are utilised to render them invisible.

Against these has been ranged the devastating armoury of the "binary" conspiracy. Traverse human history at any moment from antiquity to the present; with negligible exceptions, you will encounter this pattern of collaboration between the most powerful contending systems. They say, in effect: let us join hands to take care of these minnows so we can roam the ocean at will, not bothered by minor irritants – you take the West, we take the East. This has been the pragmatic motivation of numerous historic pacts and treaties in both major and minor keys, from the European wars of possession of the sixteenth and seventeenth centuries and the opening up of the New World, to the life-and-death struggle of capital-ism and communism that ended in a *Pyrrhic* victory for one of them. In the process, alternative models and options for the creation of a true community of man are ridiculed, vili-fied, crushed or simply driven underground.

The religious sector provides us today with the most bla-tant examples. Respect for the two "world religions" but con-tempt, or invisibility for all others. One example: the religion of Islam accepts one other, Judaism, (and its gigantesque offspring, Christianity) as a partner-rival – the absolute limits of its tolerance – since all others are regarded as offences against the Supreme Deity. Proselytisation by its arch-rival is, however, strictly forbidden, punishable by death in some nations – Afghanistan is merely the most extreme example of this familiar doctrine. To submit to conversion is equally fa-tal, since conversion is regarded as the capital crime of apos-tasy. As for the followers of all other faiths, they are obliged to convert or face permanent social exclusion, harassment and even – as in the case of members of the Ba'hai – death. It is small consolation that, despite this hegemonic pattern and its historic rampages of destructiveness, a number of little-known systems of beliefs – in Asia, Africa, the Americas or Australasia – have survived and continue to thrive. Our des-tination is one of such worlds, that of the Yoruba, where we shall arrive in a moment.

Nigeria, the nation which is home to the Yoruba, offers us a contemporary model of the effect of binary conditioning, since it was within that nation, secular in its governance from the colonial period, that a state within the nation recently declared itself a Muslim state. The immediate effect of the Islamisation of that state has been to create just such an arena between two assertive faiths, thus sucking the anterior faiths – *orisa,* ancestor or Nature worship etc. etc. – even deeper into the black hole of invisibility. It is a good instance of that theocratic binary con-trick, the elision of spiritual ver-ities that can be elicited from other religious world-views, especially of the antecedent autochthonous faiths over which these two foreign contenders have spread their imperial cloak. Predictably, the arguments have gone back and forth between the two: the legal system being practised is based on Christian law, hence we must oppose it with ours, claims the Council of Imams and their surrogates. The other, the Christian Association of Nigeria, replies in kind, determined to defend its own established turf on similar grounds, both aided and abetted by the international media whose binary conditioning is so endemic that it cannot even refer to Nigeria except in such terms as the Muslim north and the Christian south. Occasionally, in fairness, we must state that we do encounter the informed qualification of *the predominantly Moslem north* and *the largely Christian south* or other grudging variations.

The neglected truth, however, is that this state, Zamfara, like many other parts of the so-called Muslim or Christian parts of Nigeria, also consists of other religious faiths, those pre-Christian and pre-Islamic faiths that are so wishfully dismissed as mere vestigial and inconsequential paganisms. The Jukums, the Tivs, the Bornos of Northern Nigeria continue to follow (sometimes side by side with Islam or Christianity) the religions of their ancestors. So the moment a state opts to become a theocracy, no one bothers to ask: what are the pronouncements of existing traditional religions – not now of the opposing member of the binary catechism – what is the teaching of such religions on the imposition of a theocratic mandate on community, society or state? To such a question, the answer is clear: abomination!

To address one such world, that of the Yoruba, let us begin where it all begins, within human consciousness – that world repudiates the hegemonic tendency, as is demonstrable in its most fundamental aspect: the induction of a new living entity into the world and its dedication to the spiritual custody of unseen forces. A child is born. Quite early in its life, when the parents discern in this new organism traces of personality, later to become known as character (*iwa*), this newcomer is taken to the *babalawo*, the priest of divination, who adds his tutored observations to the signs that have already been noted by the parents. Sometimes, the *babalawo* takes the child through the actual divination process. Mostly however, it is his shrewd eyes, extensive experience and honed intuition that decide for him: this, he observes, is a child of Osun, or this is a child of Sango, or Obatala. It does not matter that neither parent is a follower of any such deity, or that no one in the entire household, or in the history of the family has ever been an initiate of this god. The child, it is accepted, brings his or her own *ori*, destiny, into the world. It is futile to attempt to change it or to impose a different one on him.

Yet even this allotment of the child's spiritual aura is not definitive, nor is it exclusive. Some other incidents in its life passage – a series of setbacks, a display of talent, creative or leadership precocity, or indeed some further revelation of earlier hidden traits such as a tendency towards clairvoyance, or simply the child's habit of enigmatic utterances – any of these may lead the *babalawo* to conclude that a different guardian deity is indicated for the child, or an additional one. And thus, a new deity is admitted into the household. There is no friction, no hostility. All gods, the Yoruba understand, are *manifestations* of universal phenomena of which humanity is also a part. *Ifa* is replete with *odu* – those verses that are at once morality tales and historic vignettes as they are filled with curative prescriptions. They narrate at the same time the experiences of both mortals and immortals for whom *Ifa* divined, advised, and who either chose to obey or ignore *Ifa*. The sceptics are neither penalised nor hounded by any supernatural forces. The narratives indicate that they simply go their way.

Some definitions are probably needed here. *Ifa* is the corpus of prognostic verses that interpret the future and prescribe options and directions for the seeker. These narratives have been transcribed and translated by such anthropologists as Herskovits, Bascomb, Gleason etc. and quite recently by Epega. The deities have themselves been the subject of a large body of traditional drama, very much in the manner of, but owing nothing to, Greek classic drama: *Oba Koso, Oba Waja* by Duro Ladipo, *The Imprisonment of Obatala,* by Obotunde Ijimere, *Esu Elegbara* by Wale Ogunyemi, and numerous epic narratives and the usual adventure tales. My own long poem *Ogun Abibiman* merely follows an ancient tradition, albeit turned to a contemporary political use. And of course, the medium of representation has become famous all over the world and even altered the perception habits within European painting and sculpture towards the end of the nineteenth century. In more recent times, painting and decorative motifs from architecture to fabrics have joined in the celebration (or maybe simply the exploitation) of the limitless bounty of Yoruba mythology. These reminders are not offered as validation – the Yoruba deities and their world need no validation. Our intention here is simply to emphasize that these seemingly exotic figures have been with the external world for a very long time, albeit as artistic resources, but also, as in the case of Latin America, as palpable areas of spirituality, manifested in their own right, and in their syncretic transformations with the Roman Catholic religion that was the religion of their enslavers.

Ifa, like the *orisa,* does not proselytise. *Ifa* does not anathemise non-believers; on the contrary, there are verses in *Ifa* which warn against disrespect to other religions. Of course, *Ifa* is not without its own tendency towards a little self-promotion, and so we find that *Ifa* is also filled with narratives of the headstrong and cynics who disobey the injunctions of *Ifa* and thus fall deeper and deeper into misfortunes, until they return to the original path mapped out by Orunmila. There is a crucial difference, however, in this process of cause and effect that differs from what I call the jealous religions. It is never Orunmila, the divination god of *Ifa,* or any agent of his who is responsible for their misfortunes. No, it is their *ori*, destiny, the portion that they brought with them into the world, the very definition of their being, that *Ifa* merely diagnosed before leaving them to their own devices, to their own choices. Nor is it, for instance, the resentment or vengeance of one rejected deity that proceeds to take up his or her own cause by assailing the luckless head of the unwilling acolyte; the gods remain totally indifferent to who does or does not follow them or acknowledge their place in mortal decisions.

The Yoruba understanding of the nature of Truth is indeed echoed by the Vedic texts from yet another ancient world, the Indian, which declares:

> *Wise is he who recognises that Truth is* One *and one only, but wiser still the one who accepts that Truth is called by many names, and approached from myriad routes.*

The accommodative spirit of the Yoruba gods remains the eternal bequest to a world that is riven by the spirit of intolerance, of xenophobia and suspicion.

The dominant religions of the world and their theologies as received up to the present day, have meant not the search for, or the love of, but the veneration and consolidation – at whatever cost, including torture and massacres – of propositions of truth, declared revelation. It has meant the manipulation of truth, the elevation of mere texts to dogma and absolutes, be those texts named scriptures or catechisms. This failure to see transmitted texts, with their all-too-human adumbrations, as no more than signposts, as parables that may lead the mind towards a deeper quarrying into the human condition, its contradictions and bouts of illumination, a re-examination of the phenomena of nature, of human history and human strivings, of the building of community – it is this failure that has led to the substitution of dogma for a living, dynamic spirituality. And this is where the Yoruba deities have an urgent and profound message to transmit to the rest of the world.

There is an urgency about this, as the world is increasingly being taken over by the most virulent manifestations of dogmatic allegiances, the nurturing terrain of which expands every day, and aggressively. In the twelve months since the introduction of the theocratic state in Nigeria, and as a direct consequence of this action and the escalation of intolerance in tastes, private relationships, social habits and even public associations, at least fifteen thousand lives have been lost, often in the most ghoulish manner. Hundreds of mosques and churches have been destroyed, hotels and social meeting places torched. The labour and achievements of generations have been wiped out in orchestrated mayhems, often instigated by those who claim to serve one supreme deity or the other. Neighbourliness, the sense of community, has suffered nearly irreparable harm. But the *orisa* continue to insist: leave the gods to fight their own wars. This brief voyage into the world of the *orisa,* hopefully, may challenge a few ears and eyes into embarking on a serious, sobering critique of their world.

It has become necessary to reiterate that, before Islam or Christianity invaded and subverted our world-views, before the experience of enslavement at the hands of both Arabs and Europeans, the African world did evolve its own spiritual accommodation with the unknown, did evolve its own socio-economic systems, its cohering systems of social relationships, and reproduced its own material existence within an integrated world-view. It is necessary to reiterate that those systems are still very much with us and have indeed affected both the liturgy and practice of alien religions, even to the extent of rendering them in some instances docile and domesticated. Thus, whenever in contemporary times the aggressive face of one or the other of these world religions is manifested, our recourse is primarily to the strengths of those unextinguished virtues of our antecedent faiths, the loftiest of which will be found in such attitudes as tolerance. I refer, of course, to genuine tolerance, not the nominal, rhetorical or selective kind, not tolerance as an academic exercise of comparisons, but one that is demonstrable by the very histories of the deities – their travails, errors and acts of reparation, as recorded in their mythologies – and their adaptability to the dynamic changes of the world.

Orisa is the voice, the very embodiment of tolerance. Not for one moment do I suggest that the faith that is *orisa* claims a monopoly on the virtues of tolerance – on the contrary. But the tenets of *Ifa* are governed by a frank acknowledgement of the fact that the definition of truth is a goal that is constantly being sought by humanity, that existence itself is a passage to ultimate truth, and that claimants to possession of the definitiveness of knowledge are, in fact, the greatest obstacles to its attainment. Acceptance of the elastic nature of knowledge remains *Ifa's* abiding virtue, and the spirit of tolerance is captured in this defining *odu* of *Ifa*:

> *B'omode ba nsawo ogboju, bi o ba ko ogbo awo lona, kio o gba a l'oju. Bi o ba ko agba isegun, ki o je e n'iya lopolopo. Bi o ba burinburin ti o ri agba alufa nibiti o nfi ori k'ale, ki o d'oju re de 'be. A da a f'awon alaigboran tii wipe: Ko si eniti o le mu won. Ee ti ri? Eyin ko mo pe: Ajepe aiye ko si f'omo ti o na Ogbo awo. Atelepe ko wa fun awon ti nna agba isegun. Omo ti nna agba alufa nibi ti o gbe nkirun, iku ara re lo nwa. Warawara ma ni iku idin, warawara.*

The brash youth meets an ancient *babalawo* and strikes him. He meets an old herbalist and humiliates him. He runs into a venerable Moslem priest kneeling in prayer and knocks him to the ground. *Ifa* divined for such *insolent* ones who boasted that they were beyond correction. Is that so indeed? Don't you know that a youth who strikes a priest of *Ifa* will not partake of this world for long? Premature is the death of the youth who strikes the devout imam at his devotions. Speedily comes the death of maggots, speedily.

120 **Wole Soyinka**
Playwright, poet, filmmaker and philosopher. Winner of the 1986 Nobel Prize for Literature.

Born in 1934 in Abeokuta, Nigeria. Studied literature and theatre in Ibadan und Leeds. Jailed for political reasons during the Nigerian civil war in 1967–69. Since 1994 exile in the United States and the United Kingdom as the leader of Nigerian political opposition. Charged with state treason by Nigeria's military junta in 1997. President of the International Writers' Parliament since 1997.

Selected publications: *The Man Died. Notes from Prison* (1972); *Ake: The Years of Childhood* (1981); *Isara: A Voyage around Essay* (1989); *Mandela's Earth and Other Poems* (1989); *The Open Sore of a Continent: A Personal Narrative of the Nigerian Crisis* (1996).

BERNDT OSTENDORF

THE PARADOX OF TOLERANCE

Radical citizenship postulates the integration of the immigrant 'other' regardless of race, gender, national origin and religion. This indifference towards differences represents the enlightenment heritage of classic liberalism, a widely respected constitutional practice of such immigrant societies as the United States. The safeguarding of individual freedom and of civil rights as the greatest of all possible goods has become an integral part of most liberal constitutions. And it has, inevitably, become a global dream. For the hope for freedom and liberation are powerful motives at work behind the historical drift of most societies towards institutionalized individualism and individualized life politics.

However, such indifference to difference discriminates against the men and women who *are and want to be* different, and particularly against those who, due to a history of racist, sexist or religious discrimination, have had no choice but to depend on their group for political support. Free individuals vs. strong groups, individualism vs. communitarianism – this dilemma of difference and belonging lurks at the core of the current conflict over multiculturalism. In her book *Making "All" the Difference* (1990) Martha Minow, former assistant to Supreme Court Justice Thurgood Marshall, captures the dilemma well:

When does treating people differently emphasize their differences and stigmatize or hinder them on that basis? And when does treating people the same become insensitive to their difference and likely to stigmatize or hinder them on that basis?... The stigma of difference may be recreated both by ignoring and by focusing on it.

What is preferable, to ignore all differences and insist on universal equality before the law, or to emphasize historically grown differences and to recognize these as political capital? Michael Walzer and Charles Taylor at any rate propose that multicultural societies need to nurture and respect a second good: group rights and ethnic loyalty. Next to the classic liberalism 1, they call for a multicultural liberalism 2:

The first kind of liberalism ("Liberalism 1") is committed in the strongest possible way to individual rights and, almost as a deduction from this, to a rigorously neutral state, that is, a state without cultural or religious projects or, indeed, any sort of collective goals beyond the personal freedom and the physical security, welfare, and safety of its citizens. The second kind of liberalism ("Liberalism 2") allows for a state committed to the survival and flourishing of a particular nation, culture, or religion, or of a (limited) set of nations, cultures, and religions... – so long as the basic rights of citizens who have different commitments or no such commitments at all are protected.

In other words, liberalism 1 is, in terms of culture or religion, contentless and merely guarantees the pursuit of happiness to a plurality of individual citizens. Tolerance is defined by indifference. Liberalism 2 on the other hand protects a normative idea of belonging, of the good society and the right values – usually those that have guaranteed group survival. And normative differences would require quite a different sort of tolerance, one that would ultimately be self-defeating. Liber-

alism 1 represents the classic American position of a weak and neutral state, liberalism 2 the classic German position of a strong, normative notion of belonging.

One thing is clear, liberalism 2 keeps its innocence only under the stern vigilance of liberalism 1. A politics of difference respecting race, gender, religion or national origins requires the safety net of tolerance held in place by a universal grammar. Here we run into the communitarian dilemma that not only mirrors a key problem of multiculturalism, but brings out the American or exceptionalist character of the debate: How to prevent the cultural loyalties of liberalism 2 from becoming "normative" or "essential" and how to prevent boundaries, designed to protect one minority, from being exclusive to other minorities. Can strong communities and free individuals get along? Though ethnic cultures and racial boundaries based on endowment are by any classic anthropological definition normative, how can they be made voluntary? Here we have, in Goethe's words, *des Pudels Kern,* the core of the multicultural dilemma and its solution: the balance (or imbalance) between the freedom and necessity of belonging to a community. Tolerance ranges between the poles of positive or negative indifference or positive or negative loyalty. And here the European and American stories diverge.

Some theorists like John Rawls have argued that both the defense and the abolition of difference is an essential part of an unending sociogenesis which unfolds as a negotiation between inevitably particularistic communities within an inevitably universalistic liberal state. When he calls the United States a "nation of nations" it follows that the former (nation) has to be taken with a universal, the latter with a particularistic spin. This dual orientation sounds balanced in theory. How does it work in practice and how do tacit assumptions in the American and German public cultures control or affect the meaning of such differences and boundaries? In the United States liberalism 1 ruled supreme from 1789 to the 1980s. The American debate on multiculturalism reacts to that dominance with a "new liberalism" that would respect group rights. In Germany liberalism 2 was taken for granted until very recently. Here the multicultural mobilization serves to strengthen liberalism 1. Hence both the historical wounds and their therapies are at cross-purposes. At this juncture a first cognitive dissonance between Germany and America appears in the political and historical semantics of difference. Not only does the ethnic "other" have a specific historical ring in Germany, but the two radical options, separatism vs. integration, are grounded in different pragmatic, political force fields. In short, the national debates on multiculturalism, though apparently similar in their rhetoric and surface goals, react to and work over different historical wounds. In Germany the hidden choreography of the debate is defined by the defeat of liberalism after 1848 and by the antiliberalism of the Nazis which ended with the Holocaust, the most radical politics of difference imaginable. In Germany "to make a difference" stands in the shadow of *Sonderbehandlung, Endlösung* or more recently *Fremdenfeindlichkeit*. This is part of our national, historical legacy. Hence politically conscious Germans are loath to consider a politics of ethnic or cultural difference as a "countervailing" balance to a politics of integration and assimilation. With an eye on the failure of liberalism after 1848 and the Holocaust they argue for complete legal equality, that is, for liberalism 1.

In the United States the public debate works over conflicting experiences: the co-existence of both the success and the failure of liberalism for different groups. The success of liberalism for white males is paired with the wounds of slavery for Blacks, with the legacy of colonialism for Native Americans and Hispanics and of sexism for women. In America the quest of ethnic groups for a politics of difference and cultural autonomy had a positive and a negative motive. After the liberal principle of individual civil rights was achieved in the courts (1954–1965), the economic and social opportunities for African Americans, Native Americans and Hispanics did not improve as expected. Full political citizenship, Blacks were first to find out, did not protect them against social or economic discrimination. Such victims of discrimination needed help not as individual American citizens but as members of discriminated groups. The affirmative step was to transfer the principle of equal rights from the individual to ethnic groups. This positive push for a recognition of group rights was reinforced by a negative reaction towards the corrosive effects of a possessive individualism on the one hand and the stultifying process of Americanization and mass cultural homogenization on the other.

Since difference in any immigrant society is inevitable, Americans turned the vice of difference into a virtue of commodification. The squaring of the circle, as it were, was found in a binary switch. Divisive, negative ascriptions were changed by an act of consciousness-raising into a positive identity, expressed in ethnic markers such as Afro hairstyles or in bumper stickers with "Black is beautiful", or songs such as "Say it loud, I am black and proud", a transformation which worked remarkably well, albeit more effectively in the culture industry than in social relations. The formerly negative recognition of difference was transvaluated by an act of consciousness-raising into the recognition of positive difference. This was ground for celebration and gave a boost to the ethnic market. A popular bestseller trumpeted the good news: *I'm ok, you're ok*. Consequently, when the belief in the equality of individuals was applied to groups, this led inevitably to the assumption that all cultures must be accepted on an equal footing as basically good. European observers might want to quote Nietzsche's warning that a tolerance that tolerates everything becomes contentless. But this is precisely the secret power of the American marketplace. Herbert Marcuse called its ability to turn difference into profit "repressive tolerance". This secret talent of the American public order is anchored in the tradition of voluntarism codified in the first amendment. We can begin at the beginning and quote the

Mayflower contract, which was "voluntarily agreed upon". Voluntarism was a key concept of the Federalist Papers and flourished in the early republic, when individuals flexed their muscles and exercized their new freedoms guaranteed in the constitution and the amendments. German conservatives have always marveled at the self-help organizations and the much more inclusive definition of the private sector, and our Left successfully imported civil disobedience and *Bürgerinitiativen* (citizens' initiatives) in the late 1960s. Many voluntary associations of the private sector, let me hasten to add, are too often stabilized by Social Darwinist advantages such as money, family status, chauvinism and racism. No wonder that Social Darwinism as a social philosophy for the selection of the fittest was so successful in America. Therefore Germans will tend to characterize the American principle of freedom as hypocritical, since it is embedded in Social Darwinist practice. But the point I want to make is that the cultural principle of voluntarism is so deeply embedded in the American unconscious and in daily political practice that it is simply taken for granted as being god-given and natural, even by the American Left. It is telling that the communitarians, who desire a return to normative values, insist that the change in the habits of the heart should be voluntary.

Even ethnicity, the ultimate determinant of identity by descent, has come under the sway of voluntarism. Mary C. Water's *Ethnic Options – Choosing Identities in America* concludes that "ethnicity is increasingly a personal choice of whether to be ethnic at all... it matters only in voluntary ways... First, I believe it stems from two contradictory desires in the American character: a quest for community on the one hand and a desire for individuality on the other." But this liberal option must be legally available in order for voluntarism to work. She quotes the official instructions for the census takers for the 1990 census: "List the ethnic group with which the person *identifies*". How did that voluntary option get into the instructions for a census which is supposed to form the solid statistical rock for policy making? Through voluntary associations, in this case through the active lobbying on the part of *white* ethnic leaders in Washington. There is an interesting process at work here. The essentialist or primordial quality of descent acquires, in the American political process (that is, in the free exercise of individual rights), an exceptional or voluntaristic quality, a privilege, I repeat, which extends primarily to white ethnics. You cannot choose not to be black though this has been tried close to the colour line with the tradition of "passing".

Translated back into the political process, however, such voluntaristic ethnicity becomes essential again (in both meanings) when the division of political spoils along an ethnic or a colour line, as in affirmative gerrymandering or quotas, has to be administered and defended as public policy. Voluntary ethnicity recoups its normative losses in democratic proceduralism under the given patterns of inequality of the market. This curious process of voluntary de-essentialization and procedural or juridical re-essentialization is, I believe, the cause of much of the resentment among white ethnic males in America and explains the current crisis of affirmative action in the public sphere.

Quite clearly African and Native Americans have not enjoyed the privilege of voluntarizing community. They had no choice or wanted no choice. Continued racism was the dividing line between voluntary white and involuntary non-white ethnicity. Indeed, racism kept African and Native American communities and community bonding alive. Hence the sense of community among African and Native Americans has an "Un-American", almost German ring to it, one reason, perhaps, why there seems to be an elective affinity between community-oriented Germans and African or Native Americans. This compensatory role of community as an antidote to the structural racism within American liberalism explains why the "white male ethnic" American Michael Walzer, who enjoys the privilege of voluntary options, has no choice but to

128 consider the protection of minority-community, that is, of people without such options, a "liberal" cause. This idea, I submit, is not exportable to Europe without losing its liberal innocence.

This repressive tolerance of de-essentialization may best be explained by looking at another facet of the American political creed: the role of religion in the political public sphere and the separation of church and state along the lines of voluntarism. I suspect that the voluntarization of ethnicity is modeled on the manner in which primordial religious loyalties (as expressed in the dictum "una sancta catholica" or "once a Jew always a Jew") were denominationalized. Denominationalism, which has by this time become a deep seated political faith, is the American way of pulling the political teeth of religious passions as envisaged in Federalist 10. The two parts of this crucial compromise on religious difference are set down in the first amendment, in the two freedoms "from and to": first, the free exercise clause grants each individual the freedom to exercise his/her religious faith without interference from the state and from other individuals and, as a consequence, the anti-establishment clause aims to prevent the rise of any sort of unique ecclesiastic, dogmatic or institutional religious power. Hence America has no *ecclesia,* no state church, and no institutional religious power. The power-sharing between church and state – typical of the *Konkordat* (of June 1933) between the German government and the Vatican – is to the average American decidedly the work of the devil. Not surprisingly, American denominations are notoriously weak on dogma, but high on general morality or on principles of a civic religion. Not surprisingly, even political parties in America are weak on "program" and strong on mobilization. In the course of American history the organisation of ethnic difference has fallen in line: the *free exercise* of ethnic difference is widely accepted, but most Americans, including members of ethnic groups, are hesitant, if not wary, of the *establishment* of ethnic difference as a political power.

Hence the current crisis of affirmative action or of governmental set-aside programs is not surprising. Interestingly, ethnic elites want it more than the rank and file, for they tend to find jobs in the management of ethnic politics.

Since our focus is difference, we can now differentiate between denominational ethnicity which continues to be accepted and "established" or "dogmatic" ethnicity that has so far failed to convince a clear majority of Americans, even of African Americans. A preference for a denominational ethnicity is borne out by a poll, entitled "What Ordinary Americans Think about Multiculturalism", conducted in the early nineties among the most postmodern, poststructuralist and in my view least ordinary, Americans, namely Southern Californians:

> *We have found that the mass public* – more or less irrespective of ethnicity – *is sympathetic to culturally diverse groups. There is a respectful recognition of diverse heritages. But there is little mass support, at this time, for official recognition of these ethnic differences or for special entitlements attached to them. And this lack of mass support for particularistic multiculturalism holds despite much* more supportive elite rhetoric *and official policy both in California generally and in the Los Angeles area.* (my emphasis)

Germany has no first amendment tradition for the domestication of religious difference. But while Germans have accepted the institutional empowerment of the church in the *Konkordat,* they take revenge in freely exercising their right of not going to church and of not confusing personal morality and political talent. Yet, without a first amendment no liberal constitutional tradition exists for de-essentializing difference, whereas difference in Germany remains inescapably *essential.* Indeed the discourse on the "politics of difference" along the boundary lines of *Gemeinschaft* has an almost exclusively right-wing tradition in Germany. This fact was brought home to me when I presented current American theories of multi-

130 culturalism (Richard Taylor, Martha Minow, Iris Marion Young, Michael Walzer) to the members of the City Council of Munich, which included at the time the right-wing *Republikaner*. The person most interested in Walzer's liberalism 2 turned out to be the press secretary of the *Republikaner*, who welcomed this unexpected support for his party's platform from the American deconstructionist Left. Therefore those historically conscious Germans are correct who argue that multiculturalism is but a half-way house to an enlightened citizenship law and to a political culture honoring consent, not descent, a position that we have yet to reach. Hard multiculturalism of the Walzer kind is entirely compatible with our right wing's efforts to keep the difference between Germans and *Gastarbeiter* intact. The press secretary of the *Republikaner* would gladly import the more radical politics of difference of Taylor, Young and Minow to Germany as a compromise which would allow him to exercise a modicum of *Fremdenfeindlichkeit* without running the risk of being *verfassungsfeindlich*. Indeed the multicultural model of a politics of difference or of an "ecological protection of diversity" has been proposed by some members of the CDU whose notion of a *Leitkultur* sets the boundaries of admission along the lines of cultural difference. American freedom, on the other hand, is, in Isaiah Berlin's classic definition, a "freedom from interference of the state" and a "freedom to do your own thing", and these freedoms inevitably shape ethnic or cultural co-existence. In America the state should be weak and inactive, the individual strong and active; in Germany, where the state has a history of being strong and active, the individual tends to be weak and inactive. This continues to be a habit of the heart across political divides. Without voluntarism even a small difference can, in Sigmund Freud's assessment of the Balkans, become narcissistic – and deadly.

Berndt Ostendorf 131

Professor of American Cultural History at the Ludwig-Max-imilian University, Munich.

Born in 1940 in Oldenburg, Germany. Studied in Freiburg (Ph. D. 1968), Pennsylvania and Glasgow. Professor of American Studies at University of Frankfurt 1976–81; Guest professor in New York, Boston, New Orleans, Venice.

Selected publications: *Ghettoliteratur: Zur Literatur ethnischer, marginaler und unterdrückter Gruppen in Amerika* (1982); *Black Literature in White America* (1983); *Die Vereinigten Staaten von Amerika* (2, 1992). *Die multikulturelle Gesellschaft: Modell Amerika?* (1994).

Felix Unger

Tolerance and Tolerances

A Scientific Perspective

To orient itself and cope with life, mankind makes use of all the academic disciplines. Each individual is unique and stands alone in the world; he has to discover the world for himself and make his way in it. He is dependent on the knowledge and experience of his fellows. This knowledge and experience is gained from confronting life, and is then shared. The more wisdom we accumulate from all possible sources in any particular instance, the more confident we can be that the wisdom holds true, and the more solid it becomes as a foundation we can build on. We are all familiar with this process, which allows us all to recognise that "red" is "red".

Congruent experience can be used to develop common starting points from which to acquire new knowledge, which, in turn, forms the starting point for yet more new knowledge. We use measuring techniques to objectify our knowledge. These techniques make ever more accurate descriptions and comparisons possible whilst also permitting their weighting and, not least, evaluation. The more objective knowledge becomes, the more a specific item of knowledge is generally accepted, the stronger is its claim to be true.

We experience the world "through a glass darkly" during a very short period of time; we have to plunge into it and grapple with its problems. We can do this only by applying knowledge that is already available. In this way, we develop a closer relationship to nature than we would if our observations were based solely on our own limited experience or knowledge. As a result, however, we decipher nature with the knowledge that comes, in part, from the past, and redesign it for the future. This wealth of experience is identified and characterised by the natural, technical and environmental sciences. The latter, in particular, open our eyes to the extent to which we have already altered nature.

Theories point to further ways of analysing nature, and increase our knowledge by leaps and bounds. This all happens, however, to the detriment of individual insights or discoveries. For, as the acquisition of knowledge accelerates, the sell-by dates of current theories draw ever nearer. Nowadays theories become outdated as quickly as fashions in clothes.

Academic disciplines such as history, linguistics, economics, social sciences, jurisprudence, political science, psychology and also medicine emerge from interpersonal relations. In the most ideal cases, these sciences cull conclusions from man's rich experience, gained over thousands of years, and are able then to offer guidelines for further co-existence. Many a finding from long ago is still valid today and will remain so into the unforeseeable future. Here, there are no limiting sell-by dates.

In an attempt to sort out his life, man experiences his existential relationship to the spiritual. He experiences the transcendental; he sets off on a journey into the transcendent. This is triggered by such questions as: Who are you? Where do you come from? Where are you going? These questions have been asked and addressed since time immemorial, and not just by philosophy, the arts and religions. As these perceptions or worlds of knowledge feed on the experience of the existential transcendent and the transcendent, they change very little over the passage of time. Socrates, Abraham, Moses, Christ, Mohammed, Buddha, Plato, Aristotle, Mozart and Leonardo all found words and forms to express eternal life.

When we measure, weigh and compare, we often come up with individual values that vary from each other, but not by much; they are clustered close together. In this situation, we refer to the "tolerance" arising from the sensitivities connected with measuring or even from the measuring procedures and techniques themselves. The fact that we always have to put up with "tolerances" even in the most accurate measurements indicates that tolerance is a universal phenomenon. Nothing within nature is so crystal clear that it can be captured without tolerances. The smaller the standard deviation, the more precise and objective the measurement, and the higher degree of general acceptance. And yet the path to understanding is a long one; it takes a long time for a general recognition to be accepted as certain and true. Standard deviation is limited in natural sciences, but it quickly widens when the focus is on judging living things and becomes even wider when the focus is on evaluating spiritual issues.

In this sense, each measurement and each assertion possesses an element of imprecision, i.e. tolerance. In the exact mathematical sciences, we include a tolerance limit when we evaluate something. The entity evaluated makes a further comparison with another such entity possible, and prepares the ground for reliable discoveries and conclusions. Everyday life demonstrates the scope of the truly fantastic scientific achievements we experience, from the conquering of space to the mastering of our genes. In interpersonal relations, however, the tolerance limit is stretched much further, almost frighteningly so when such human behaviour as the performance of a doctor or the rulings of a judge is being evaluated. All too often it is practically impossible to define how far something has deviated from the norm, since no norms exist. How much further, then, is tolerance stretched when an attempt is made to apply the multitude of possible interpretations to spiritual matters, particularly when certain knowledge becomes an article of faith, and particularly when we refer to the Creator in our attempt to judge our guilt and sins in the mirror of redemption.

It always becomes problematic and fundamentalist when individuals or groups cling unconditionally to supposed truths. This is one of the origins of war. Which is why tolerance is so crucial to survival. It should train us to find certainty in estimating the range of measurements and values, and thus enable us to tread the narrow path between perspicacity and carping. The epic poems come to mind in this context. Nothing on this Earth is absolute except death; everything disintegrates in the pulse of life.

In the field of genetic engineering, scientific progress has made it possible to chart life's fundamental code as an alphabet of life. Reduced to the basics, the life of each human being is founded on four amino acids (C,A,T,G), the sequences of which permit incredible variety over the centuries of human existence. Everything is a variance of the One. There is no plurality in life, merely variations on the One. Each one of us is a unique variant of the One that cannot be reproduced. There is no duplication, not even through cloning. The time factor and the surroundings prevent this from happening.

Tolerance is in our genes. Our approach to evaluating the mean variations, elements of imprecision and bandwidths in life is, moreover, a result of our upbringing. We keep making value judgements: usable, unusable, good or bad. In doing so, we build up our personal existential protection, while at the same time we create the lever that gives us access to our neighbour. Thus, living together with others will always stand in relation to life's central values. Tolerance helps us to co-exist and is ultimately bound to the fundamental values of life. It is a virtue.

Within the framework of the interdisciplinary interplay of all sciences, of inter-religious dialogue and of mankind's need for orientation, tolerance can be interpreted as the motor that drives interpersonal relationships, as something that is not just in our blood, so to speak, but already lies dormant in our genes.

In the same way as we develop and absorb science by means of measuring, comparing and evaluating, we must develop tolerance in our lives. All knowledge comes complete with an element of imprecision, and the smaller the range of variation, the more certain is our knowledge. The European Academy of Sciences and Arts has approached the subject of tolerance within the scope of a broad interdisciplinary discourse. It has developed a charter of tolerance on the basis of real life, which ultimately stands in relation to the fundamental values of our life. It helps us all to live together across the globe, and is therefore of pivotal importance. We must make every effort not to be self-righteous.

Just as each one of us has to discover the Earth for ourselves, it is always up to each one of us to decide how to deal with others and with nature. Our stance must be firm to ensure that lack of precision does not dissolve into uncertainty. Tolerance is present at all levels of human knowledge. Closer, tangible limits in our relationship to nature are easier to grasp and they enrich our lives. The limits are stretched when it comes to interpersonal relationships and even more so when it comes to the spiritual domain. The limits and imprecision arise from the variance of life. Only if each individual makes the effort to respond to the variance of life and marks out the limits of tolerance can we ensure peaceful co-existence throughout the world.

Tolerance opens our eyes to life and our hearts to our neighbours.

Felix Unger

Heart surgeon and university professor. President of the European Academy of Sciences and Arts in Salzburg.

Born in 1946 in Klagenfurt, Austria. Studied medicine in Vienna; trained as a cardiologist and surgeon; extensive training as a heart surgeon in the United States. Medical superintendent of the public hospitals in Salzburg since 1986. Cofounded the European Academy of Sciences and Arts in 1990; president of the Academy since 1991. Numerous medical publications.

Seamus Dunn

The Slow Path to Mutual Understanding

Tolerance, according to Paul Ricoeur, is "a tricky subject: too easy or too difficult."[1] That is to say, the meaning of the term is either clear and simple and obvious, or it is profoundly complex and impossible to define in any generally agreed way. An examination of the available sources of information and literature about the term will support this view, and will indicate both an absence of conceptual clarity, and the potential within the term for vagueness and confusion. A search of the Internet provides some understanding of the very large number of relevant documents and materials currently available, and will add to this sense of imprecision. Clearly, however, tolerance is a matter of great interest and concern for many, and consequently there is a continuing need for analysis, interpretation and elaboration of its range of meanings and its applicability, especially in the light of such contemporary phenomena as racism, xenophobia, fundamentalism and inter-group conflict.

Common sense meanings of the word range from "putting up with opinions and behaviour that one does not necessarily agree with", to "accepting the possibility that opinions and behaviour, different from our own, may well be right". Distinctions such as these have led to complex philosophical discussions down the centuries, and cannot be examined in any detail here.

However, because of the vastly increased complexity of the modern world, a world that often seems to be outside the control of any individual or even any government,[2] the word tolerance has become prominent and has taken on a great many contextual shades and colours of meaning. The break-up of the Soviet empire in 1991 produced an avalanche of unanticipated change and social confusion, leading to conflict, wars and human disasters, and added to the sense that democracy and civilisation were endangered by conflict and violence. In addition, the phenomena associated with globalisation, such as electronics-based communication systems, the international world of scientific and technological development, economic globalisation, and the frightening phenomenon of global warming, all contributed to the sense of new international patterns and configurations. The implications of these for our understanding and practice of tolerance are not yet clear, nor is it clear that past attempts to promote and encourage tolerance have been particularly successful.

Perhaps of more direct relevance for how tolerance can be understood and practised are the complex social and economic changes that have taken place within traditionally stable societies, both in the West and elsewhere. These changes have removed many certainties, and have produced widespread feelings of insecurity and unease. They have contributed to the generation of a range of social revolutions, including a general transformation of religious beliefs and practices, along with complex shifts in traditional understandings of the role of the family, women, marriage and of the community generally. The rise of fundamentalism within many communities and states can be linked to the insecurities, along with a sense of loss of moral and spiritual certainties, created by these changes.[3]

In addition, a growing awareness of the evident inequalities between the rich West and the rest of the world has led to (among other things) complex, widespread and seemingly inevitable patterns of economic migration. An immediate effect on Western societies of the arrival and growth of these new ethnic or minority communities has been to create strains, but they have also served to indicate that modern cultures cannot live in isolation, and that cultures inevitably overlap and interact with each other. All of these developments bring the question of tolerance into direct focus, as a signal of the need for social processes that will allow such change and diversity to be managed, accepted and welcomed.

Within the discourse that has ensued there exists a range of inter-related words and ideas, all arising out of attempts to establish a rational and cumulative approach to the creation – or re-creation – of societies where conflict and inter-group hostility can be minimised. Concepts such as democracy, human rights, pluralism, citizenship, multiculturalism and tolerance have been adopted at one time or another, especially in relation to education, as the talismanic notion that might help to produce appropriate and creative programmes and activities.

It has always been a problem for human beings, whatever the circumstances, to learn to live with each other in peace and without violence. This is true even when those involved look like each other, speak the same language, worship in the same way – that is, know each other well. This universal human difficulty has, empirically, been likely to be even more pronounced when there are obvious distinctions such as religion, skin colour, language or culture. It is clearly not an easy or a normal matter for many people to accept such differences with equanimity, and the result is often a practice of intolerance that is socially and personally dysfunctional. Overcoming such difficulties has not always proved to be impossible, however, and circumstances, training or experience can produce the structures and practices necessary for pluralist societies to function in peaceful and productive ways. Nevertheless, it is also the case that, whatever the society or the circumstances, intolerance will always exist and will never disappear completely.

A great many historical contexts can be examined in which both the absence and the presence of tolerance have been evident. For example, the absence of – or a reduction in – tolerance can often be found where the society is relatively volatile or unstable because of political, social, economic or demographic change. In such conditions there is often competition for resources, employment or levels of power, or just a degree of uncertainty, insecurity or stress caused by unfamiliar circumstances, or a fear of the unknown.

Conversely, the presence of tolerance usually accompanies a settled, secure, or balanced arrangement, where the society is stable and changing in a controlled or measured way, the population is homogeneous, and the various population groups have become known to each other, are comfortable with and trust each other, and are not in direct competition in their everyday activities.

Power relationships within society are obviously of particular importance. Those not in power will often have little option other than to tolerate (that is "endure") the demands of those with power, and to hope that if they are sufficiently subservient and agreeable they will themselves be tolerated. When the society is well established and stable, then these different forms of tolerance may have advantages for both groups. Conversely, when the circumstances produce intolerance, it will normally take some time for the high costs of this intolerance to be recognised. This recognition is often the first step in the pragmatic search for procedures and structures that can create tolerance.

However, neither the presence of tolerance or intolerance is guaranteed: when circumstances change and existing stresses disappear or new stresses emerge, then the existing levels and degrees of tolerance are themselves likely to change accordingly. That is to say that the process of going away from tolerance, or coming to tolerance, has to do with social and demographic change, shifting relationships and the diversity of cultural beliefs present within the community. The

142 pessimistic view is that social diversity in the modern world is growing so fast that peaceful ways of adapting to it are often beyond our immediate capacity.

This leads to the question as to whether the process of coming to tolerance can be generated or strengthened within a society through such means as education, and, if so, how this is best accomplished. One way into this discussion is to examine how the subject of tolerance has been written about by international organisations. We can begin with the United Nations itself. The Preamble to the UN Charter assumes that the word tolerance is well-defined, and so refers to the importance of reaffirming "faith in fundamental human rights, in the dignity and worth of the human person, ... and for these ends to practise tolerance and live together in peace with one another as good neighbours". This of course is a worthy aspiration and from such a source has some significance, but it has very limited immediate applicability. How is it to be achieved? The Universal Declaration of Human Rights is hardly more precise, placing tolerance in the realm of education, with the view that education "should promote understanding, tolerance and friendship among all nations, racial or religious groups" (Article 26).

The year 1995 was designated as the *United Nations Year for Tolerance* and this meant that a considerable quantity of related material was produced, and emphasis was placed on the importance of education as a medium for the promotion of tolerance. UNESCO was given responsibility for the "Year" and produced a "Declaration of Principles on Tolerance" with a long definition of tolerance in four parts. All these are quite general, and are essentially descriptive declarations of principle: for this reason they are difficult to summarise and provide little immediate assistance for the generation of practical activities and programmes. This of course may be inevitable given the constraints on programmes created by particular contexts.

Numerous societies for whom education is thought to be

an important way of trying to deal with the problems of racism, fundamentalism and intolerance have faced (and are facing) the difficult task of designing and implementing suitable and relevant educational programmes. School systems all over the world have been trying to establish and maintain such programmes, with the aim of contributing to the promotion among young people of the ideals of tolerance, democracy and good citizenship. Comprehensive research about these worldwide programmes remains to be carried out, but it is clear that their content varies considerably depending on a number of contextual constraints and circumstances, and so it is difficult to provide a coherent and structured analysis that does justice to their complexity.

The major classificatory variable in such an analysis is the country or region in which a project is based, and its individual history and experience of intolerance, including discrimination, divisions based on nationalisms, violence, imperialism, dictatorship and so on. Some examples of categories (which inevitably overlap) are now outlined, but this is not intended to be other than a first step in this process.

In some regions the problem is very old, resulting from a historical division of the population into two or more communities or ethnic groups that often claim different nationalities and have difficulty in living peacefully with each other. This usually results from a long-term and fundamental experience of difference, such as language, skin colour, ethnicity or religion, and very often there are also economic differentials of an extreme kind. Examples include Northern Ireland, Sri Lanka, Israel-Palestine, the Basque Country and South Africa. In these situations education, where it can become involved at all, has the task of promoting mutual understanding between the groups, and emphasising the importance and value of diversity, and the long-term advantages of democracy and citizenship.

A second category results from ideological conflicts, often in formerly colonised states, with a deprived and downtrodden underclass which may be composed of a range of ethnic groupings. Such states may pass through a stage of dictator-ship or military rule with many state-related killings and dra-conian laws. The process of emerging from this into democ-racy often involves attempts to use education as a way of bringing the peoples together, to indicate the power and in-fluence of democracy, and to propose ways of moving away from intolerance and inter-group strife. Examples include South American states such as Chile and Brazil, and African states such as Nigeria and Kenya.

In other cases the problem is the result of long-term inward migration where people from other societies either voluntar-ily or involuntarily (as in the case with African Americans) move to live in another state. Examples include America, Australia, Japan and Great Britain. Such circumstances usu-ally produce debates about the creation of a single nation, cultural assimilation and state-building, and related educa-tional programmes have often reflected this in the past. More recently the emphasis is more likely to be on multiculturalism and respect for ethnic pluralism and diversity.

A fourth category relates to the situation where the migra-tion patterns are more recent, and where the migrants are from quite different linguistic, religious or ethnic groups, and have arrived in large numbers. Examples include Chicanos in America, Pakistanis in Great Britain, Turks in Germany and North Africans in France. In these cases the problems for minorities of discrimination and intolerance can be extreme, and are often compounded by unemployment, low wages and poor housing. Again the educational emphasis in such cir-cumstances is likely to be on cultural pluralism, respect for cultural differences and a widening of the curriculum.

Finally, there is the situation to be found following the fall of a failed or extreme political regime, sometimes in the con-text of war or revolution. This often involves a breakdown in what was previously an enforced uniformity, and the resur-facing of suppressed differences. Possible examples here in-clude some of the countries of the former Soviet Union.

This wide range of categories means that, for now, generalisation will be difficult: however some understanding may be possible through the medium of case-studies, such as the following brief survey of relevant educational developments within Northern Ireland. The Northern Ireland government was established in 1920 and contained within its boundaries two distinct communities: first, a Catholic/nationalist group associating itself with an Irish tradition and culture; and, second, a Protestant/unionist group associating itself with a British tradition. The two groups therefore had different constitutional aspirations, and to this end each developed its own set of institutional forms, including separate educational systems.

The renewal of widespread violence between the two communities in the late 1960s stimulated a long debate about the impact of these separate schools on relations between the two communities. Since then many voluntary and NGO groups have worked from the assumption that educating children apart must have some negative impact on their adult perceptions and attitudes, and that trying to establish a better understanding and more contact must be helpful. Two programmes have emerged out of this attempt at education for tolerance. The smaller and more radical movement has sought structural change in the system, especially the establishment of integrated schools where Protestant and Catholic children can be educated together. The other approach has adopted a programme called Education for Mutual Understanding (EMU) with the aim of providing programmes within the existing denominationally segregated schools.

Both these programmes came together formally in 1989 when new legislation was enacted, which moved this work out of the informal and voluntary sphere. The new law made it incumbent upon the state to encourage the development of integrated education, where feasible, and made EMU a part of the statutory curriculum in all state funded schools. It defined EMU as follows:

Education for Mutual Understanding is about self-respect and respect for others, and the improvement of relationships between people of differing cultural traditions. The overall goals of the programme include enabling pupils to learn to respect and value themselves and others; to appreciate the interdependence of people within society; to know about and understand what is shared as well as what is different about their cultural traditions; and to appreciate how conflict may be handled in non-violent ways.

EMU was designated as a "Cross-Curricular Theme", a status it shares with a number of other themes such as Health Education. Such themes are to be taught within other subjects, and EMU is frequently integrated into subjects such as history, religious education or literature. It is also intended that they can include non-curricular approaches such as peer mediation and joint or inter-school activities such as dramatic productions.

The lessons to be learned from this experiment are not as yet clear. Not all research results about outcomes have been totally convincing, but there is some evidence that, at least in some contexts, changes are taking place. Certainly the idea that education has a role to play is now more widely accepted within the community than ever before.

It is of great importance that attempts are now made to develop systems of judgement and evaluation about the quality and success of such programmes and about how they can learn from and interact with each other at an international level, and so learn from each other and adapt and change accordingly.

1 Paul Ricoeur (editor), *Tolerance between Intolerance and the Intolerable,* 1997.
2 Anthony Giddens, *Runaway World: How Globalisation is Reshaping our Lives,* London, 1999.
3 K. Peter Fritzsche, "Citizens under Stress: An Explanation for Xenophobia", in: Russel F. Farnan et al. (editors), *Tolerance in Transition,* Bibliotheks- und Informationssystem, Oldenburg, 2001.

Seamus Dunn
Professor, Centre for the Study of Conflict, University of Ulster, Coleraine.

Born in 1939 in Northern Ireland. Studied mathematics, then conflict research at the University of Ulster. Headed the Centre for Conflict Research from 1988–1999, specialised in education-related issues and political, social and historic dimensions of the conflict in Northern Ireland. Recently conducted international research on "Pluralism in Education" and "Minorities in Education."

Selected publications: *Integrated Schools in Northern Ireland* (1986); *A History of Education in Northern Ireland Since 1920* (1990); *The Role of Education in Conflict Societies Education for Peace* (1991); *Ethnic Minorities in Northern Ireland* (co-author in 1997).

Yoram Kaniuk

Boundless Tolerance belongs in Heaven

In most European languages, the term "tolerance" stands for correct, non-discriminating social intercourse between people, with mutual respect for different opinions. At the same time the term, which derives from the Latin "tolerare", may denote a capacity for enduring pain or misfortune. In English, for example, the term is used simultaneously as an expression to show mutual respect and as a medical term as in the following: "Induction of oral tolerance as a treatment of inflammatory bowel disorder."

The Hebrew term *sovlanut* – tolerance – is a neologism which doesn't appear in biblical sources. The newly-created word derives from the root *saval*, which is also the origin of *savlanut* – patience. To express the capacity to endure pain, Hebrew has other terms. *Sovlanut* is used solely to mean toleration of one's fellow-man, allowing him to live according to his own will and beliefs, to think and to express himself the way he wants. The conviction that respect is due to the right of one's neighbour to express himself the way he likes is firmly rooted in this enlightened world of ours. This privilege is conceded to everybody, be (s)he a crank, a choleric or an eccentric. Most liberal thinking human beings on this planet are at least aware of the respect principle: there is no higher good than freedom of speech. But unbridled freedom of speech for every individual doesn't work – in the interests of society, it must be subject to subtle limits. Society has to accept this if it wants to be not just nice, but also prudent. In other words, if society is interested in its own survival.

Even the first approach to the term "tolerance" proves to be difficult if we do not hide behind that enlightened concept, "political correctness". A democracy has the moral and legal obligation to protect the opinion of a minority. But with respect to freedom of opinion and speech, it would be inaccurate to state that in the course of the last thousand years or so, the civilised values of the West have become absolute values because they are – according to Western societies – of greater significance than the values observed by inferior societies. However beautiful the spontaneous song of the native may be – it will never come near Beethoven's Ninth Symphony. But where freedom of speech is concerned, it is not possible to provide an absolute aesthetic yardstick, and this in itself already contains a certain measure of intolerance. What is good and what is less good? According to what standards can values be determined in the case of those who accept neither God nor a leader to decide on their behalf? Some standards of culture have been accepted as universally valid. Not everything is equally good, hence not everything is relative. One can safely say that a play by Shakespeare or Beckett is of greater importance than a comedy show, no matter how funny and successful the show may be. Entertainment as an end in itself is to be judged by entertainment criteria, while artistic values are subject to different standards.

Tolerance – accepted as one of the highest values in Western societies – cannot in the moment of truth tolerate someone who is striving to eliminate it. Today millions of Muslims support Osama bin Laden, whom they regard as a charismatic leader. But those advocating tolerance in Western societies will have great difficulty accepting a view which endangers their very existence. The French philosopher Voltaire once declared that he was prepared to die for everyone's right to the freedom of opinion. But what about the opinion that the attack on the Twin Towers in New York was a deed in the name of god and a requirement of Jihad, the holy war against the infidels?

Tolerance is indissolubly connected with freedom of speech, with religious freedom and the right to be different from others. Tolerance protects a social or ideological minority against their being overwhelmed by the majority. Democracy has to protect such a person whom Henrik Ibsen calls an "enemy of the people". But should freedom of opinion and speech be placed higher in the value hierarchy than a society's right to exist when this is put into question by those freely expressed opinions? Once again the answer is ambiguous, except, of course, to those who claim the superiority of their own right to freedom of speech with such fanatic radicalism that the principle of freedom is itself perverted. Thus the freedom-of-speech-and-opinion right of every individual, and not just of radicals and extremists, has to have limits put on it, since nothing leads more consistently to dictatorship than the proclamation of an absolute truth and the firm belief in it.

In Denmark, freedom of speech and opinion is highly regarded. So highly that most copies of the infamous "Protocols of the Elders of Zion" are printed in Denmark as are other anti-Semitic writings of the worst kind denying the Holocaust. In Germany, despite all concern for freedom of speech, there are severe restrictions on the publishing of racist, radical right-wing material. But in Denmark, only racism is outlawed. So what should a Dane do if he is on the one hand enlightened and upright but at the same time wants to make money? Simple enough: he sells his books and pamphlets legally printed in Denmark to other European states where publication of Nazi-material threatening to incite public disorder is legally prohibited.

Should tolerance accept forms of intolerance – indeed, is it even obliged to do so? Do I have to respect – in the name of tolerance – a person whose intention it is to demolish the pantheon of tolerance? In totalitarian states where one person decides what is right and what is not, ethics and morality do not exist. This problem arises only in democracies. Terms such as "freedom" and "peace" have become ideals. But the question remains as to whether freedom includes allowing robbery and murder to be committed as long as they are committed in the name of freedom and in a society other than my own. This double moral standard has been part of Western civilisation for a long time. For years and years, Western thinkers generally considered to be enlightened justified what took place in the Soviet Union, playing down the genocide committed by Stalin and his henchmen, the biggest act of enslavement since Hitler's reign of terror. They justified the slaughter by ignoring it or by interpreting it as a transitional step towards a better tomorrow. And even when they looked, they managed to see nothing. When they read Bucharin, André Gide and Arthur Koestler, all of whom returned from Stalin's realm and exposed what was really going there, the vast majority of these intellectuals, the champions of boundless tolerance in their own societies, refused to understand. They were blinded by lofty phrases such as "tomorrow's world" or "the peace camp". When Albert Camus spoke out against the crimes committed by Stalin's regime, he was villified by the French left. When socialists from all over Europe enthusiastically went to Spain to crusade against the dictator Franco, Stalin's men dogged their heels and murdered all those who showed any sign of disloyalty to the party line. Picasso's dove of peace, which united millions throughout the world who believed in progress, peace and tolerance against the transgressions of capitalism was banned in the Soviet Union – as an anti-communist work of art. But at the same time, unbeknownst to the genius who created it, it served as a fig leaf for Stalin's regime of terror, a wall behind which the communists committed million-fold murder.

152

Absolute tolerance, no matter how important it may appear as a basis of human civilisation, has not existed in the past, nor will it do so in the future. Picture the following, for example: in Germany of 1923, a man comes to a publisher and presents him with a manuscript entitled *Mein Kampf*. In this manuscript, the publisher learns about a planned genocide. His liberal stance is put to a severe test: if indeed he publishes the work, he may be contributing to a future mass murder. However, he is respecting freedom of speech and the writer's opinions even if they are admittedly radical. Or he decides not to tolerate the opinions of the man called Adolf Hitler, who, by voicing his ideas, is abusing freedom of speech. By refusing to publish Hitler's concoction, the publisher violates Voltaire's principle; he is being proactive, demonstrating a form of intolerance that arises from the need to act defensively when confronted by incitement to murder and conversion by force. Yes, he might be harming Voltaire's legacy – and Voltaire would certainly have modified his principle had he known about a work such as Hitler's *Mein Kampf* – and is going in the face of political correctness. But by refusing to publish the manuscript, the publisher accepts that a human life – even the life of a Jew – is of greater value than a principle when it supports the kind of dogmatic fanaticism that negates moral behaviour.

The fact that in Hebrew "tolerance" – *sovlanut* – and "patience" – *savlanut* – are so closely related makes me think of a less extreme situation than the one above: I am driving in my car (I don't have one, but let's assume I do) through Tel Aviv. In the passenger's seat I have a person who is mortally ill. I have to get him to hospital as fast as possible. The man is groaning in pain. There is another car just ahead of me. The driver is a nice person who is being polite by giving the right of way to all other cars, making it impossible for me to get to the street I need. Because I am a patient person, I wait. But the man next to me is about to die. So I honk discreetly. Then a little less discreetly. The nice person in front of me gives me a dirty look. He wants to teach me how to become an exemplary citizen like himself. There is no way for me to overtake him. I'm stuck. Finally I jump out of my car, insist that he allow me to pass, return to my car and overtake him. The man will definitely think that I am an intolerant road hog, completely lacking in patience. But I am about to save a man's life.

Intolerance, therefore, may serve as a measure of defence especially for those who stand up for the ideal of tolerance. As a matter of fact, we need to relativise terms we consider sacred and, depending on the situation, subject them to conscious choice. We have to protect ourselves against all kinds of dogmatism, since seemingly unselfish goodness often conceals a considerable measure of cunning. Tolerance towards someone who doesn't simply hold an opinion different from mine but also intends to destroy me is no virtue. It is merely proof of stupidity. Boundless tolerance may exist in heaven; it is hard to put it into practice in this world of ours. For all that tolerance appears to be a marvellous, desirable and enlightened concept, it is not always appropriate. Each of us has to judge. Absolute values exist only in dictatorial and theocratic regimes. Nonetheless, the belief in absolute values such as tolerance has never diminished.

Tolerance is a good thing. It is not part of the world of tomorrow proclaimed by Stalin. It is a part of a world which is too far away from ours ever to be reached. But just as the Jews are still awaiting the Messiah, knowing deep in their hearts that He will not come, we have to stick to the principle of tolerance, while at the same time keeping our scepticism and our wariness. In a democratic society with its relative liberalism, each of us has to decide every moment anew what is right and what is not. Only in religion, in totalitarian regimes, are there any absolute truths. Or in the Garden of Eden, where Adam obediently did what he was told. But the moment he tasted the forbidden fruit and his eyes were opened, he was driven out of Paradise. Now he knew what he was forbidden to know. Now he could distinguish between good and evil without God controlling and directing him. From then on, man had to decide for himself what was right and what was not, what was good and what was evil. Christianity calls this eating from the Tree of Knowledge and the subsequent punishment – having to decide in a cognitive indeterminate framework what is permitted and what not – original sin. The Jewish view is different: Jews claim that "everything is determined and permission given": Everything is determined from Above, but man still has to make his choices. For this reason Moses could say: "Who comes next to You among the deities, my Lord?" Or as the Jewish bible says: "Everything is given by GOD, except the fear of GOD." What is permitted and what is forbidden is always the individual's choice with respect to a fixed set of values. Kierkegaard describes the choosing individual as an ethical subject; he claims that ethics always involve conscious choice while moral principles derive from traditional rules established by human beings. Tolerance becomes a goal worth striving for only when it is consciously chosen by someone who has to decide what is right and what is wrong. After having been awarded the Nobelprize for literature, Albert Camus was speaking to students in Stockholm when he was reproached by an Algerian student for not supporting an independent state of Algeria. Camus replied that on the one hand France had to fight Islamic terror. But on the other, Algeria should belong to both the French and the Algerian people.

In saying this, I feel a little uneasy. I have always condemned terror. I have no choice but to condemn blind terror because one day it could hit my mother or my family. I believe in justice, but I will put my mother ahead of justice. She means more to me than justice for terrorists.

Yoram Kaniuk

Award-winning writer, artist, author of children's books.

Born in 1930 in Tel Aviv, Israel. Winner of the President's Prize, the Prix des Droits de l'Homme, and the Brenner Prize, Israel's highest literary award.

Selected publications: *Adam Resurrected* (2000); *Commander of the Exodus* (2000).

SLAVOJ ŽIŽEK

AGAINST A FALSE TOLERANCE

Editor's preface: The following article contains Lacanian/ Marxist/Kierkegaardian/Kantian vocabulary not immediately accessible to the philosophically uninitiated. This use of such jargon – and the philosophy behind it– does not impede a superficial reading. The reader should be aware, however, that in incorporating concepts such as "obscene", "the Other", "jouissance", "alienation", "abstraction", "real", "objet petit a" and "false" (to name but a few), Slavoj Žižek is juggling philosophies and playing with weighty concepts which he and others have written volumes on.

During an anti-apartheid demonstration in the old South Africa, a troop of white policemen was dispersing and pursuing black demonstrators. One policemen was running after a black lady, a rubber truncheon in his hand. Unexpectedly, the lady lost one of her shoes; automatically obeying his "good manners", the policeman picked up the shoe and gave it to her. At that moment, they exchanged glances and both became aware of the inanity of their situation – after the gentlemanly gesture of handing her back the lost shoe and waiting for her to put it on again, it was simply IMPOSSIBLE for him to continue running after her and to hit her with the truncheon. So, after politely nodding at her, the policeman turned around and walked away… The moral of this story is NOT that the policeman suddenly discovered his innate goodness – we are NOT dealing here with a case of natural goodness winning out over racist ideological training. On the contrary, in all probability the policeman was and remained a standard racist. What triumphed here was simply his "superficial" training in politeness.

When the policeman stretched out his hand to return the shoe, the gesture was more than a moment of physical contact. The white policeman and the black lady lived in two different socio-symbolic universes with no direct communication possible. For each, the barrier between the two universes was for a brief moment suspended, and it was as if a hand from another, spectral, universe reached into ordinary reality. However, in order to transform this magical suspension of symbolic barriers into a more substantial achievement, something more is needed – such as, for example, the sharing of obscene jokes. In former Yugoslavia, jokes caricaturing a specific characteristic of the various ethnic groups used to circulate freely. Montenegrins were supposed to be extremely lazy, Bosnians stupid, Macedonians thieving, Slovenes thrifty… Significantly, these jokes waned with the rise of ethnic tensions in the late 1980s; none were heard in 1990, when the hostilities erupted. Far from being simply racist, these jokes (especially those in which members of different nationalities meet: "A Slovene, Serb and Albanian went shopping, and…") confirmed the existence of the official "brotherhood and unity" of Tito's Yugoslavia. In this case, the shared obscene jokes did not exclude the others who were not "in", but included them, establishing a minimum symbolic pact. Native Americans smoke the proverbial pipe of peace, while we from the more primitive Balkans have to exchange obscenities. The true danger of this strategy resides in the fact that such obscene solidarity may be at the expense of a third party: for example, the solidarity of male-bonding at the expense of women. To establish actual solidarity, the shared experience of high culture is not enough; one has to exchange with the Other the embarrassing idiosyncrasy of the intimacy of obscene enjoyment.

When we share a common space with foreigners, when, for example, a delivery man or a repair man enters our apartment, we politely ignore each other to avoid encroaching on the other's privacy. The Lacanian big Other is, among other things, one of the names for this Wall which enables us to maintain the proper distance, guaranteeing that the other's proximity will not overwhelm us. When we talk with a clerk, we "do not get personal". There is a paradox here: this Wall is not simply negative; it also generates fantasies about what lurks behind it, about what the Other really desires. Our late-capitalist daily life involves an unprecedented disavowal of the Others' experience: in order to pass a homeless person crouched in a doorway and keep walking, in order to enjoy dinner when children are hungry, in order to rest at night when suffering is all around us, we have to systematically foreclose our affections for, and connections with, others. In the words of the dominant culture, our economy is comprised of individuals who respect each other's individuality. As Marx figured out, we are not dealing here with individual psychology, but with capitalist subjectivity as a form of abstraction inscribed in and determined by the very nexus of "objective" social relations. When Kierkegaard located the ultimate evil of modernity in the reign of the anonymous Public sustained by the press (daily newspapers), his violent criticism targeted the same abstraction: "The abstraction of the press (since the press is no political concretion and only an individual in an abstract sense) combined with the passionlessness and reflectiveness of the age, gives birth to that abstraction's phantom, the Public." That is to say, "abstraction" for Kierkegaard is here also "real": not just a theoretical designation, but one which applies to actual life-experience itself, the way individuals relate to themselves when they "discuss problems" from the non-engaged position of an external observer – in this case, we "abstract" ourselves from our embeddedness in a concrete situation.

So, within the market economy, abstraction is inscribed into the very individual experience. A worker experiences his particular profession as a contingent actualisation of his abstract capacity to work, not as an organic component of his personality; an "alienated" lover experiences his sexual partner as a contingent fill-in that once satisfied his need for sexual and/or emotional gratification, etc. This is how, at the most immediate level, we relate to others: we IGNORE them in a fundamental sense of the term, reducing them to bearers of abstract social functions. And, of course, this fundamental "coldness" of the late capitalist subject is supplanted and concealed by the phantom of a rich private emotional life which serves as a fantasy screen protecting us from the shattering experience of the Real of Others' suffering. Today, the old joke about a rich man ordering his servant to "Throw out this destitute beggar – I am such a tender person that I cannot bear to see people suffering!" is more appropriate then ever. The necessary price paid for this abstraction is that the very sphere of privacy gets "reified", turned into a domain of calculated satisfactions. Is there anything more depressingly anti-erotic than the proverbial appeal of a yuppie to his partner, "Let's spend some quality time together"? No wonder, then, that the obverse of this distance is the brutal and humiliating intrusions into the Others' intimate space: from confessionary talk-shows to cam-websites, where we can observe people defecating from the bottom of the toilet bowl.

Under late capitalism, then, our affective life is thus thoroughly split. On the one hand, there is the sphere of "privacy", of intimate islands of emotional sincerity and intense engagements which, precisely, serve as obstacles which blind us to larger forms of suffering; on the other hand, there is the screen (metaphoric and literal) through which we perceive this larger suffering. We are bombarded daily with TV reports on ethnic cleansing, rapes, tortures, natural catastrophes, all horrors which evoke our deep sympathy and sometimes move us to engage ourselves in humanitarian activities. But even when this engagement is quasi-"personalized" (like the photo and letter from a child in Africa whom we support through regular financial contributions), ultimately the payment here retains its fundamental subjective function isolated by psychoanalysis. We give money in order to keep the suffering others at a proper distance, thereby allowing ourselves to indulge in emotional sympathy without endangering our safe isolation from their reality. This humanitarianism-at-a-distance is the truth of the discourse of victimization: me (the harassed one) versus others (in the Third World or the homeless in our cities) with whom I sympathize from afar.

In the feel-good antiracism of the *Guess Who's Coming to Dinner* kind, the black fiancé of the white upper-middle class girl is educated, rich, etc., his only flaw being the colour of his skin. It is easy for the girl's parents to overcome the barrier and love SUCH a "neighbour". However, what about the proverbial African-American in Spike Lee's *Do the Right Thing* who annoys the whites by walking around with his boombox turned up loud? It is THIS excessive and intrusive *jouissance* that one should learn to tolerate – is he not the ideal subject of "cultural harassment"? And isn't the obsession about "sexual harassment" also a form of intolerance – or "zero tolerance", to use the popular Orwellian term of the law enforcers – of the other's enjoyment? This enjoyment is by definition excessive – every attempt to define its "proper measure" fails, since sexual seduction and proposal are as such intrusive, disturbing. Taking this to its logical conclusion, isn't the ultimate goal of the struggle against "harassment" the protection of each individual's right to be LEFT ALONE BY HIS OR HER NEIGHBOURS, protected from their intrusive *jouissance*? The courts in most Western societies freely issue "orders of restraint": when someone sues another person for harassment (for stalking, making undesired sexual advances, etc.), the harasser can be legally prohibited from intentionally coming within 100 yards of the victim. Necessary as this restraining measure is, it nonetheless contravenes the Real of the Other's desire. Is it not obvious that there is something dreadfully violent about openly displaying one's passion to the object of that passion? Passion by definition hurts its object, even if it is accepted: the receiver inevitably experiences a moment of awe and surprise.

Does this not also apply to the growing prohibition against smoking? First, all offices were declared "smoke-free," then airline flights, then restaurants, then airports, then bars, then private clubs, then many campuses... In a unique case of pedagogical censorship, reminding us of the famous Stalinist practice of retouching the photos of nomenklatura, the U. S. Postal Service eradicated the cigarette from stamps bearing photos of blues guitarist Robert Johnson and of Jackson Pollock. And there have been recent attempts to ban lighting up on the sidewalk or in a park. Christopher Hitchens was right to point out the extreme shakiness of the medical evidence against passive smoking; he claimed that these prohibitions themselves, intended "for our own good", are "fundamentally illogical, presaging a supervised world in which we'll live painlessly, safely – and tediously". Do these prohibitions not target yet again the Other's excessive, risky *jouissance,* embodied in the act of "irresponsibly" lighting a cigarette and inhaling deeply with unabashed pleasure (whereas Clintonite yuppies do it without inhaling, have sex without penetration, eat food without fat)? What's more, the notion of the danger of "passive smoking" is clearly part of the post-AIDS fear not only of direct physical contact with others, but also of the more ethereal forms of contact – the "invisible" exchange of fluids, bacteria, viruses... What makes smoking such an ideal target is that the proverbial "smoking gun" is easy to target here, and provides a politically correct "enemy" (the large tobacco companies), thus disguising envy of the Other's enjoyment in an acceptable anti-corporate clout. The ultimate

162   irony of the whole prohibition campaign is that not only have the profits of tobacco companies continued to climb, but that much of the billions of dollars the tobacco companies have agreed to pay will go to the medico-pharmaceutical industrial complex, which is the single strongest industrial complex in the United States, twice as strong as the infamous military industrial complex.

In the magnificent chapter II C of his *Works Of Love*, Kierkegaard develops the claim that the ideal neighbour whom we are admonished to love can only be a dead one. His line of reasoning is surprisingly simple and consistent: whereas poets and lovers choose their love object for his/her distinguishing features and unique outstanding qualities, "to love one's neighbour means equality": "forsake all distinctions so that you can love your neighbour". However, it is only in death that all distinctions disappear: "Death erases all distinctions, but preference is always related to distinctions". A further consequence of this reasoning is the crucial distinction between two perfections: the perfection of the object of love and the perfection of love itself. The love of a lover, poet or friend contains a perfection which belongs to its object, and is, for this very reason, imperfect love. We should, however, love our neighbour, and "since one's neighbour is every man, unconditionally every man, all distinctions are removed from the object. Therefore genuine love is recognizable by this, that its object is without any of the more definite qualifications of difference, which means that this love is recognizable only by love. Is not this the highest perfection?"

To put it in Kant's terms: what Kierkegaard tries to articulate here are the contours of a non-pathological love, of a love which would be independent of its (contingent) object, a love which (again, to paraphrase Kant's definition of moral duty) is not motivated by its determinate object, but by the mere FORM of love – I love for the sake of love itself, not for the sake of what distinguishes its object. The implication of this stance is thus weird, if not outright morbid: the perfect love is THOROUGHLY INDIFFERENT TOWARDS THE BELOVED OBJECT. No wonder then that Kierkegaard was so obsessed with the figure of Don Juan: for surely Kierkegaard's Christian love for one's neighbour and Don Juan's serial seductions share this crucial indifference towards the object. For Don Juan, the quality of the seduced object did not matter: the ultimate point of Leporello's long list of conquests, which categorizes them according to their characteristics (age, nationality, physical features), is that these characteristic don't count – the only thing that matters is the length of the list. Doesn't this make Don Juan the ultimate Christian seducer, since his conquests were "pure", non-pathological in the Kantian sense, chosen for no particular reason rather than for any particular attribute? The poet's preferred love object is also a dead person (paradigmatically the beloved woman): he needs her to be dead in order to articulate his mourning in his poetry (or, as in the case of courtly love poetry, a living woman is elevated to the status of a monstrous Thing). The poet is fixated on the singular dead love object; the Christian treats the still living neighbour as already dead, erasing his or her distinctive qualities. The dead neighbour means: the neighbour deprived of the annoying excess of *jouissance* which makes him/her unbearable. It is thus clear where Kierkegaard cheats: he tries to sell us as the authentic, difficult act of love what is effectively an escape from the effort of authentic love. Love for a dead neighbour is an easy feat: it basks in its own perfection, indifferent towards its object. But what about not only "tolerating", but loving the Other ON ACCOUNT OF HIS/HER VERY IMPERFECTION? Lacan's name for this "imperfection", for the obstacle which MAKES ME love someone, is *objet petit a*, the "pathological" tic which makes him/her unique. In authentic love, I love the Other not simply as alive, but on account of the very troubling excess of life in him or her. Even common wisdom is somehow aware of this: as they say, there is something cold in perfect beauty. One admires it, but one falls in love with

164   IMPERFECT beauty precisely because of the imperfection. For many Americans, there is something too cold about Claudia Schiffer's perfection: it is somehow easier to fall in love with Cindy Crawford on account of her very small imperfection (the famous tiny mole close to her lip).

Is this love for the dead neighbour really just Kierkegaard's theological idiosyncrasy? On a recent visit to San Francisco, while listening to a blues CD at a friend's apartment, I unfortunately commented: "Judging by the colour of her voice, the singer is definitely black. Strange, then, that she has such a German sounding name – Nina." Of course, I was immediately admonished for political incorrectness: one should not associate someone's ethnic identity with a physical feature or a name, because all this just bolsters racial clichés and prejudices. When I asked how then we should identify ethnic belonging, I got a clear and radical answer: in no way, and by means of no particular feature, because every such identification is potentially oppressive by constraining a person to his or her particular identity... is this not a perfect contemporary example of what Kierkegaard had in mind? One should love one's neighbours (African-Americans, in this case) only insofar as they are implicitly deprived of all their particular characteristics – in short, only insofar as they are treated as already dead. What about loving them FOR the unique sharp-melancholic quality of their voices, FOR the amazing libidinal combinatorics of their names (the leader of the anti-racist movement in France two decades ago was named Harlem Desir!), that is to say, FOR the idiosyncrasy of their modes of *jouissance*?

Slavoj Žižek
Philosopher and psychoanalyst.

Born in 1949 in Ljubljana. Studied philosophy and sociology in Ljubljana (Ph. D. in 1981) and psychoanalysis in Paris (Ph. D. in 1985). Visiting professor at Princeton, Columbia University, New School of Social Research, and other U. S. universities. Senior Researcher at the Kulturwissenschaftliches Institut, Essen, and Senior Researcher at the Department of Philosophy, University of Ljubljana, Slovenia.

Selected publications: *On Belief* (2001); *Did Somebody Say Totalitarianism?* (2001); *Liebe deinen Nächsten? Nein, Danke!* (1999); *Die gnadenlose Liebe* (2001); *Ein Plädoyer für die Intoleranz* (2001).

WOLFGANG SCHÄUBLE

AN ORDER WHICH BINDS US

"Whenever someone somewhere in the world forgets that he is not Number One, all hell breaks loose," said Bishop Reinelt in 1995 on the occasion of the 50th anniversary of the Dresden bombing raid. The recognition of our own limits protects us from making absolute claims and from hubris. The terrible events of September 11, 2001 have once again brought home to us that this recognition is a necessary prerequisite for people to co-exist peacefully.

We have all experienced existential threats and fears since September 11. Modern civilization is vulnerable, and globalisation simply highlights the differences between rich and poor, between different cultures and different religions. Globalisation and the Internet may appear to enhance transparency and open up new possibilities; however, they also increase our need for familiarity and orientation. People are living in ever-closer proximity to each other, and this in turn intensifies conflicts. The borders between countries and continents may be tumbling down, but this does not mean that familiar standards and norms which in the past have provided support and orientation should become less binding. Maintaining values and order, especially during a time of conflict, is both more difficult and more important.

One such value is respect for those who are different from us. But to respect others, people need to be able to respect themselves. In the basic commandment "love thy neighbour as thyself", the last two words are an integral component. Pluralism, freedom of speech, and cultural diversity require that we be tolerant of other opinions and ideologies – and we can do this only if we are sure of own views and firm in our convictions.

A social order that protects freedom, human dignity and human rights always remains vulnerable, yet it enables us to live and work together. We all have a yen for freedom, but a liberal social order also needs law as a framework. Freedom cannot be boundless.

Because freedom requires responsibility, our legal order, too, is based on the responsibility borne by each individual. If you recall some of the debates on criminal law during the 1970s, you will see how this principle clashes with the interpretation that reduces criminal law to an attempt at re-socialisation. Freedom and responsibility always require personal autonomy and self-determination of an individual.

An entire political platform can be derived from human dignity, freedom, responsibility and compassion. Liberté, Egalité, Fraternité – the triade of values of the French Revolution can be found unchanged or only very slightly altered in the declarations of principles proclaimed by modern democracies.

If social co-existence should be predicated not on regimentation, control and force, but rather on freedom, then we need a setting which allows such co-existence to function in freedom and voluntary integration. A liberal, pluralistic state can go only so far in creating such a setting, since the moment it tries to impose conditions (however beneficial), it becomes less liberal. This is what Böckenförde means when he says that a liberal constitutional state thrives on conditions which it cannot create itself.

Our liberal constitutional state is based on an essentially Judeo-Christian concept of man. This concept rejects a neutrality of values and a lack of commitments. We do not subscribe to the principle "anything goes". But this concept equally categorically rejects fundamentalism. We distinguish between the Kingdom of God and the order we need in this world. We are not out to build a theocracy. Thus, man-created order based on the Judeo-Christian principle is equally acceptable to followers of other religions and to non-believers.

When he accepted the Peace Prize of the German Book Trade, in a speech entitled "Belief, Knowledge, Opening", Jürgen Habermas made a remarkable observation from the point of view of – as he put it – a "religiously unmusical" person. He claimed that the flip side of religious freedom is the pacification of ideological pluralism. The most secular society must respect the power of articulation of religious language if it does not want to sacrifice our innate and precious resource of intuition. Since personality is partly predicated on the difference between what it is and what it should be, Habermas deduces from God's image that freedom cannot exist without mutual recognition. God can remain the deity of free people only as long as they respect the absolute difference between the creator and the created.

Fundamental human equality is based on human dignity and thus provides a basis for tolerance. Each individual is unique and distinct, and is the central pillar of a social order based on human dignity, freedom and equality. The totalitarian systems of the 20th century were based on the concept of the superiority of a nation or a class: "You are nothing, the people is everything". This is incompatible with the Christian concept of man. Those who strive to build a theocracy, fundamentalists, have no truck with tolerance. On September 11, this became abundantly and appallingly clear.

Anyone who aims to triumph over fundamentalism must be confident of his own set of values. Since national bonds provide most people with a certain measure of their self-image and identity, as national bonds appear to weaken, we should make very sure that the formation of identity is not left to the opponents of our liberal-pluralistic order, to the enemies of tolerance.

National cultural bonds clearly go beyond mere constitutional patriotism, laudable as this may be. I have always feared that constitutional patriotism may be insufficient to create an identity or foster emotional integration. Identity, affiliation, patriotism are grounded in history, common memories and myths. In this respect, the roots of our constitutional patriotism do not reach very deep, and not just because our constitution is only slightly more than 50 years old. The Basic Law has undeniably created a positive social order – far better than most would have thought possible in 1949. But because of Germany's recent history, the constitution has not been enough to provide a basis for people to love their own country.

In his book *Was wird aus Deutschland?* (What will become of Germany?), Daniel Vernet wrote that constitutional patriotism must be conveyed by the nation-state. We can accept this concept from a Frenchman – and indeed, it cannot hurt to pay attention to the observations and expectations of our European neighbours. Vernet wrote in his book that Germany's partners prefer to deal with recognisable Germans rather than with faceless Europeans. In another book, *La Renaissance Alemande* (The German Renaissance), Vernet claims that "Germany is an eternal European Enigma that cannot be understood as long as Germany does not understand itself." And David Marsh asks in his book *The Germans: A People at the Crossroads*: "How should Europe trust Germany if Germany does not trust itself?"

We are not necessarily talking about pride here – the word has too many connotations. But we need to come to terms with ourselves. If a man cannot stand himself, no one will be able to stand him either. That is true for individuals and, apparently, also for entire nations.

It was the nation-state which has engendered democracy

and the rule of law. While the nation-state is certainly not the end of history, for the time being at least, it provides its population with an identity and thus, the essential basis for a social order guaranteeing human rights and tolerance, democracy and the rule of law. For all their undeniable merits, enthusiastic Europeans such as Walter Hallstein were probably wrong when they said that Europe would replace its constituent national states. Today, we are well aware that European unification will for a long time remain dependent on the bonding strength of the member nations. And for this reason we are looking for a stable equilibrium between the individual nations and Europe in our debates on a European constitution.

Nor does the process of globalisation reduce the significance of nations. Behavioural scientists such as Eibl-Eibesfeldt have taught us that the loyalties of members of an anonymous large-scale community diminish in relation to their distance from the centre. Thus, strengthened regionalism must accompany the process of European unification and globalisation. Proximity and familiarity become increasingly important when societies are in a state of flux. A world order cannot be based on unilateralism. Multilateral structures remain necessary, and recognising this, all viable forms of global governance promote identity creation.

Communities organised into a nation-state require an order which binds them. This order guarantees freedom and human dignity to everyone. Tolerance becomes possible only when each member of such a community is aware of his identity and can live with it – as an individual and as a citizen. Thus, healthy self-confidence, especially that of a nation, is not the opposite of tolerance; rather, it is the prerequisite for making life in a community lively and diverse.

Wolfgang Schäuble 171
Member of the Executive Committee of the Christian Democratic Union of Germany (CDU). Member of the German Parliament (Bundestag).

Born in 1942 in Freiburg, Germany. Studied law and economics in Freiburg and Hamburg, Ph.D. in 1971. CDU-Member since 1965. Elected to the Bundestag in 1972. Minister for Special Affairs in 1984–1989 and Interior Minister in 1989–1991. Chairman of the CDU/CSU Bundestag faction in 1991–2000. CDU Chairman in 1998–2000. Member of the CDU Executive Board since 1989. Member of the CDU Executive Committee since April 2000.

Selected publications: *Der Vertrag. Wie ich die deutsche Einheit verhandelte* (3, 1991); *50 Jahre Bundesrepublik* (co-author, 1999); *Die Politik und der Frieden. Der deutsche Beitrag zur Sicherung des Friedens* (with Javier Solana, 1999).

Jutta Limbach

THE ELEVENTH COMMANDMENT

The task of ensuring that people of very different cultures and religions co-exist in peace has occupied us to an ever greater extent in the past few years. There is a good reason for this: Germany has become a multicultural state with people of different cultures and religions living side by side – Christians and Jews, active churchgoers and passive worshippers, atheists and agnostics. While Germans in the west and east of the reunited country still have rather different attitudes and values, there are even greater cultural contrasts between Germans and immigrants from many parts of the world who have come here looking for a job, a place to study or refuge from political persecution.

Germany is the most important country of immigration after the United States. Over seven million foreigners live here. About three million of them are Muslims. An increasing diversity of cultures and religions in Germany is creating tension and conflicts. Such confrontation mostly comes into the open in school classrooms. The conflict is frequently triggered off by a religious sign or a symbolic artefact characteristic of a specific religious faith. The "Islamic headscarf" or "crucifix" discussions immediately come to mind.

The question as to whether a schoolteacher should be allowed to wear a headscarf for religious reasons during lessons has been the subject of much public controversy and has been put to the test in the courts. This discussion is not confined to Germany: the debate about headgear worn by school students for religious or traditional reasons, for example the kipa, the turban or the *foulard Islamique*, has been conducted quite intensely and has reached the highest courts in other European countries. It has recently become increasingly clear, however, that it is the Koran which demands that Muslims behave differently from or even counter to the majority of the population.

The simple suggestion that immigrant men, women and children should adapt their behaviour to the customs of their host country is pointless. Policies that require the minority to adjust itself to the demands imposed by the majority culture are hardly consistent with our constitution (the Basic Law). The majority principle is certainly an important element but it is not alone in determining the nature of our democracy. Certain basic values are also part of it. The terrible demonstration of inhumanity after the collapse of the Weimar Republic taught the authors of the German constitution that a democracy cannot function without legally enforceable fundamental rights. Our constitution begins with the declaration of the principle of the inviolability of human rights as a way of reintroducing the rule of law in response to the Holocaust and to the corruption of law by the Nazis. Thus, according to the constitution, democracy is a delicate balance between majority rule and human and civil rights.[1]

Since the constitution protects the freedom of religion, conscience and ideology, any attempt to establish intellectual or religious dominance, such as the concept of a "defining culture" implies, is out of place from the start. The freedom of convictions, based on "the right to exercise secular freedoms", opens the way for the "development of different religions and convictions."[2] The constitution does not contain any "ethical standards" in the form of maxims that have developed in today's civilised nations and condensed into matching sets of basic moral precepts. Rather, the "ethical standard" of the constitution is its openness vis-à-vis the plurality of ideologies and religions. That is what the Federal Constitutional Court explicitly states.[3]

It is incumbent upon all public authorities in Germany to respect the freedom of faith, conscience and ideological convictions and thus to observe the precept of tolerance. If tensions between majority and minority cultures arise, then the courts, in handling the complaints brought by the minority, must defy the majority if constitutional guarantees are at stake.[4]

It is true that the concept of "tolerance" is not directly referred to in the constitution. Yet legal interpretation and theory are in agreement that this principle arises out of the overall meaning of the constitution.[5] The Constitutional Court sees the precept of tolerance primarily expressed in the principle of the inviolability of human dignity. The right to free personal development, the ban on discrimination against divergent convictions, and religious freedom in Germany are solid proof that "the constitution has defined tolerance as a leading principle of liberal democracy".[6]

This was the basis of the first crucifix ruling in 1973. The Constitutional Court came to the conclusion that it cannot be expected of a Jewish lawyer and a Jewish plaintiff to have to participate in a court case when a crucifix is placed on the judge's table, as this is contrary to their religious convictions. The refusal by the judge to remove the cross as requested during the hearing violated the complainants' fundamental right to religious freedom, the Constitutional Court maintained. "The cross is regarded as a symbol of suffering and of the power of Christ and has been seen for centuries as the perfect symbolic representation of the Christian faith."[7]

If a room has a crucifix in it, then it is reasonable to assume that this testifies to a close attachment to Christian ideas. Since few people have actually objected to crucifixes in courtrooms, the Constitutional Court has not felt compelled to rule that having crucifixes in courtrooms is unconstitutional. But it was forced to rule that having to conduct a lawsuit "under the cross" was a violation of the fundamental rights of a non-Christian.[8]

Only a state that maintains neutrality in matters of faith can guarantee the peaceful co-existence of different or even conflicting religious faiths.[9] The German constitution does not permit an established church.[10] The well-being of the human soul and political power are two different things. Nevertheless, state and church are not separate in Germany in a strictly laicistic sense as is the case in France and the United States. The state may cooperate with the churches and support them in accordance with our constitution, because a liberal democracy has a vested interest in supporting the values conveyed by churches. History has shown that people whose moral standards have their roots outside the political domain are more able to oppose the abuse of power by the state. In this way, the freedom of faith and conscience is also capable of acting as a restraint to power.[11] At the same time, cooperation between church and state should not lead to the state firmly identifying itself with a specific religious community.[12]

Since we already live in a multicultural society, the state will no longer be able to limit itself to just maintaining its neutrality. Increasingly, more and more people are convinced that cultural differences are necessary and deserving of protection, or even that cultural diversity promotes the development of mankind.[13] Religious and ethnic minorities should be therefore given a chance to develop their culture and traditions. State authorities responsible for integrating different cultures must develop strategies which guarantee their peaceful co-existence without making them culturally uniform. If different lifestyles cause unavoidable tensions, then a compromise based on mutual tolerance and acceptance must be found.[14]

The solution of conflicts by courts can only be seen as the last resort. Wherever tensions appear, an attempt must be made to settle them by exercising mutual consideration. This applies primarily to schools, since xenophobia and racism are signs that education has failed to provide moral guidance. Our efforts must therefore be focused on making young people capable and ready to respect and understand those who are different from them.[15]

School education has a greater task than just developing cognitive abilities, says the Constitutional Court. School "should also help pupils develop their emotional intelligence. School activities are geared to promoting the comprehensive development of their personality, focusing particularly on the students' social behaviour."[16] Correspondingly, students should be prepared to live together with people from other cultures and to directly or indirectly further international understanding.[17] Here I agree with Böckenförde that schools in this day and age cannot be asked "to provide children with the picture of a protected, 'closed' world that in reality does no longer exist."[18] Schoolboys and schoolgirls should, if possible, already be taught in primary school that different religions exist and that their followers differ from each other in the way they think and in what they eat, drink or wear. The old adage "there's nothing like starting young", applies here too, namely, whoever wants to come to grips with the challenges of the future should adopt a cosmopolitan view early in life.

Does a teacher who wears a headscarf for religious reasons during class, display this cosmopolitan attitude? The Administrative Court of Lüneburg[19] said "yes", while the Administrative Court of Stuttgart and the Higher Administrative Court of Mannheim said "no".[20] The two Baden-Württemberg courts are concerned that children and teenagers are very impressionable, which is an important factor since a teacher usually is a role model for the students. Therefore a teacher who wears a headscarf for religious reasons during class would infringe on the basic rights of her pupils and their parents since the principle of neutrality guarantees them the right to express, even negatively, their religious convictions.[21]

Whether a headscarf, worn as an indication of religious obedience, actually produces such a signal effect as was established in the case of the crucifix, will keep the Federal Administrative Court and the Constitutional Court busy for some time. Certainly neither court will be able to ignore the fact that the European Court of Justice for Human Rights used the same arguments and came to the same conclusion as the two Baden-Württemberg courts.[22] This development has made it more difficult for the German courts to find the right arguments, but it does not rule out the possibility of their reaching a verdict of their own based on the most recent developments in the academic debate on this subject and thus once again of providing a new impetus to the deliberations on this issue among international legal experts. The European Court of Justice admits that it is difficult to evaluate precisely the influence of a headscarf on the freedom of conscience and religion among younger children.[23]

The behaviour of a religious minority should not go against other basic values of our constitution. This could be the case if religious artefacts represent a symbol of oppression and thus offend against the bearer's or the pupils' sense of dignity and liberty. The constitution also guarantees that men and women are equal. Yet one cannot simply interpret the headscarf worn for religious reasons as a symbol of oppression or as an expression of a fundamentalist attitude. However, a veil that only allows a woman's eyes to be seen, while covering the rest of the head, could be judged differently.[24]

Extreme caution must be displayed in each individual case when searching for the right balance between the teacher's and the children's religious beliefs as well as taking parental rights into consideration. A number of objective circumstances have to be taken into account such as whether the teacher in question is just one of many teachers at a primary school or whether she is the class teacher. Very much also depends on whether the teacher's personality can guarantee that children are not subjected to religious indoctrination.[25] And,

178   not least, special attention must be paid to the teacher's ability to practise tolerance, since she, as a member of a minority, should be tolerant of those whose convictions differ from hers.

Living together in a multicultural state has become more difficult following the events of September 11. Those terrorist attacks were an assault on an open and free society. That act has brutally undermined the rational basis for the need to separate church and state and has contributed to the growing fear of religious fundamentalism. It has slowed the search for differences between Islam and Islamism and has weakened the readiness to tolerate those of different religious convictions. This was precisely the terrorists' perfidious purpose: to scare people into surrendering their civic virtues.

But intolerance and rejection of foreign cultures can provide no positive answers to the acts of barbaric terrorism. If an open society wants to win out against terrorism, it cannot allow itself to be led astray in its observation of basic values. It is the declaration of the inviolability of human dignity and the free development of personality that makes democracy so distinctly different from totalitarian ideologies. So, in order to keep this distinction alive, it is becoming increasingly vital to win people's hearts and minds in the dialogue between cultures.

Notes

1 Aharon Barak, *Judicial Discretion*, New Haven 1989, p. 129.
2 Ernst-Wolfgang Böckenförde, "'Kopftuchstreit' auf richtigem Weg?", in: *Neue Juristische Wochenschrift*, Heft 10, 2001, pp. 723, 724.
3 BVerfGE (Federal Constitutional Court) 41, 29 (50).
4 Ronald Dworkin, "Gleichheit, Demokratie und die Verfassung: Wir, das Volk und die Richter", in: Ulrich K. Preuß (ed.), *Zum Begriff der Verfassung*, Frankfurt am Main 1994, p. 172.
5 Böckenförde, see above, S. 726; Gottfried Leder, Religionsfreiheit und Toleranz, in: *Toleranz und Religion, Perspektiven zum interreligiösen Gespräch*, Hildesheim 1996, pp. 151, 153.

6 BVerfGE 35, 23 (32).

7 BVerfGE 35, 366 (374).

8 BVerfGE 35, 366 (375).

9 BVerfGE 93, 1 (16).

10 Art. 140 GG (German Constitution) together with Art. 137 paragr. 1 Weim. Verf. (Weimar Constitution).

11 Martin Morlok, in: Horst Dreier (Hrsg.), *Grundgesetz-Kommentar*, Bd. I, 1996, Art. 4 Rn. 25.

12 BVerfGE 44, 103; 93, 1 (17).

13 At its 31st General Assembly in Paris, UNESCO adopted an unprecedented document: a declaration on protecting global cultural diversity. *Süddeutsche Zeitung*, 6. 11. 2001, p. 15.

14 Böckenförde, see above (fn. 2), p. 725.

15 See, for instance, Ludwig Liegle, referring to Schleiermacher, "Das Verstehen und die Achtung des Fremden als Aufgabe von Bildung und Erziehung und als Lernprozess", in: *Neue Sammlung*, Vierteljahres-Zeitschrift für Erziehung und Gesellschaft, 1998, pp. 357, 359.

16 BVerfGE 93, 1 (20).

17 Best explained in Böckenförde, see above p. 725, who is referring to the ruling by the Lüneburg Administrative Court of 16. 10. 2000, in: *Neue Juristische Wochenschrift* 2001, Heft 10, pp. 767, 769.

18 Böckenförde, see above, p. 726.

19 See above, fn. 17.

20 See the ruling by the Stuttgart Adminstrative Court of 24. 3. 2000, in: *Neue Zeitschrift für Verwaltungsrecht* 2000, 959. See the ruling by the Higher Administrative Court of Mannheim of 26. 2. 2001, in: *Neue Juristische Wochenschrift* 2001, Heft 3, pp. 2899.

21 So says the Higher Administrative Court of Mannheim, see above, fn. 20, p. 2903.

22 European Court of Human Rights, ruling of 15. 2. 2001, in: *Neue Juristische Wochenschrift* 2001, Heft 39, pp. 2871.

23 ECHR, see above, fn. 22, p. 2873.

24 Cf. a very detailed review by Ernst-Gottfried Mahrenholz of the issue "Darf die Schulverwaltung einer Schülerin das Tragen eines Schleiers in der Schule verbieten?", in: *Recht der Jugend und des Bildungswesens* 1998, pp. 287.

25 Cf. a very appropriate interpretation by the Lüneburg Administrative Court, see above, p. 770.

180 Jutta Limbach
Lawyer. President of the German Federal Constitutional Court

Born in 1934 in Berlin. Studied law in Berlin. Professor of Law at the Free University, Berlin, in 1972. Professor of Law and Sociology at the University of Heidelberg in 1974. Headed the Department of Justice in Berlin's Senate in 1989. President of the Federal Constitutional Court since September 1994. Several controversial legal decisions have been reached during her tenure: "Soldiers-Are-Killers"-Verdict, "The Crucifix"-Verdict, "Right-to-Asylum"-Verdict, "Old-Age-Pensions"-Verdict.

Selected publications: *Im Namen des Volkes. Macht und Verantwortung der Richter* (1999); *Das Bundesverfassungsgericht* (2001).

RAINER MÜNZ

THE PROBLEMATIC STATUS OF ETHNIC MINORITIES IN GERMANY

It was not until the 19th century that Germany became a modern state based on national-ethnic principles. The idea was that all those who identified with the German language and culture should live together in a single state rather than in a dozen principalities. It was this idea that drove people to the barricades in 1848. And, of course, it was out of the question that Germans should live under the yoke of "foreign" princes or peoples, so Prussia and Austria went to war with Denmark in 1864 to "free" the German-speaking population of Schleswig-Holstein. The same guiding principle was also one of the causes of the war of 1870–71 against France. In the aftermath of the war, the newly-formed German nation-state annexed the German-speaking Alsace and parts of Lorraine, even though most people living in the Alsace did not see themselves as Germans.

Under the emperors Wilhelm I and Wilhelm II, Germany was a constitutional state but it was hardly a tolerant state, as can be seen in its policy towards minorities. While the fate of German-speaking minorities abroad was a natural cause for concern with calls for local autonomy, the freedom of cultural identity, and even for a revision of national borders, there was no comparable policy vis-à-vis ethnic and religious minorities at home. On the contrary, from the end of the 19th century on, Prussia pursued a clearly defined strategy of political discrimination aimed at undermining the cultural identity of its Polish-speaking and other minorities. Its goal was obvious: such ethnic groups should first be assimilated and then disappear. In addition, Bismark's Germany viewed Jews and Catholics as well as Social Democrats and trade unionists as enemies of the state. This provided fertile ground out of which an entire gallery of enemies of the Nazi state were later to be created: Jews, Slavs, Catholics, Social Democrats and communists. This was not logically inevitable but certainly historically predicated. People belonging to these groups were persecuted, displaced, enslaved as forced labourers, or simply murdered.

Following the military defeat of the Nazi regime, two German states arose in 1949 in the shadow of the Holocaust: West Germany and the GDR. Through the forced assimilation, displacement and extermination of the Slavs, Jews, Roma and members of other ethnic minorities, the populations of both German states were ethnically highly homogenous. In addition, the subsequent departure of former prisoners of concentration camps and forced labourers in the late 1940s and early 1950s made both nations practically "free of foreigners", if we disregard the presence of the Allied forces stationed there.

The state formed in western Germany in 1949 created a society with the most liberal constitution (the Basic Law) that had ever existed on German territory. But in formulating the concept of the German nation and its citizens, the authors of the new constitution were applying the status quo defined by the Nazi policies of racial persecution. Accordingly, a citizen of the Federal Republic of Germany was someone who had already had (or still had) German citizenship in 1945 or was admitted into the country as an ethnic German refugee. This made it painfully clear whose claim to German citizenship was going to be rejected: Jews who had fled or been driven out of the country, political opponents of the Nazi regime who had been stripped of their citizenship, and the so-called "displaced persons", namely the former inmates of Germany's concentration and forced labour camps who had remained in the country because they couldn't or wouldn't go back to their own countries.

Thus, Germany's Basic Law did not and does not provide any rights for minorities similar to those which Western states are now trying to introduce in Central and Eastern Europe and in the Balkans. In 1948–49, the framers of the constitution saw no obvious ethnic or ethnic-religious minorities who had to be protected. The Sorbs in the Lausitz region were not on the agenda since they lived in the Soviet occupation zone, even though the Basic Law did not explicitly limit its jurisdiction to the three areas occupied by the Allied troops. The rights of the Sorbs, a Slavic ethnic group, were finally defined in 1991 by the constitutions of the regional states of Saxony and Brandenburg. A Danish minority in Schleswig-Holstein also enjoys a special status, negotiated in 1954 by a state treaty between Bonn and Copenhagen. Currently two more minority groups are recognised in Germany: Frisian Germans and Roma gypsies.

All these groups enjoy a so-called "traditionally settled" status, which is awarded to minorities who have lived in the country for centuries. They are given the sort of ethno-cultural protection reserved for a rare species. This status means that their existence is not simply tolerated but is actively supported and encouraged. For example, the use of the Sorbian or Danish language is allowed in select public kindergartens and schools in areas where ethnic Sorbs and Danes live; the languages are used in public broadcasting; public funds are provided to run ethnically orientated theatres, dance groups, choirs and cultural associations. The five-percent voting threshold has been waived for the Voter Association of Southern Schleswig in Schleswig-Holstein in order to allow the Danish minority to have political representation at the local level and in the state parliament.

This waiver of the five-percent clause shows that the rights of a minority group do not depend on its relative or absolute size. Today all the "traditionally settled" minority groups taken together add up to fewer than 200,000 people. At the same time, more than 7.3 million foreigners and well over a million naturalised German citizens who were born abroad live in Germany. Many of them are, in fact, also members of ethnic or ethno-religious minority groups. They belong to what are referred to as ethnic "communities". Yet, legally speaking, they cannot claim any kind of minority status, since they have not been "traditionally settled", but have either immigrated or were born in immigrant families. This situation is clearly politically motivated.

The need for a change in the Basic Law has been a topic of discussion in Germany since the country's re-unification in 1990. A draft of an article to regulate the rights of minorities was put forward, but nothing was decided. Many members of the German parliament and experts on the subject expressed fears that not only would the Sorbs, Frisians, ethnic Danes and the Roma claim their legal right to the subsidized preservation and promotion of their cultural identity, but first- or second-generation immigrant Turks, Kurds, Serbs, Italians and Kosovo Albanians as well as naturalised Germans who had been born abroad as well. The majority of parliamentarians dealing with the issue did not want this to happen, nor did they want the matter to be decided by the Federal Constitutional Court. This is why the German Basic Law continues to have no clause on the rights of minorities. The fruitless debate was going on just as we were busy trying to convince all the newly-formed nations in Europe – from Estonia to Macedonia – how important it was to protect the rights of minorities. It was going on at the same time as we were getting deeply involved in defending the rights of German-speaking minorities in Kazakhstan, Russia, Poland and Romania.

As far as Constitutional Law goes, the situation in Germany is quite clear. While the religions, languages and cultures of its foreign and naturalised citizens are tolerated, there is no legislation ensuring their protection or promotion. In this particular aspect Germany is quite different from such countries as Canada, the United Kingdom and Holland, whose policies on minorities take immigrants and their children into account.

The consequences are well-known. If you have a stereo TV and live in the transmission area of the Mitteldeutsche Rundfunk, you can watch children's cartoons in Sorbian. Yet the 2 million-plus people in Germany whose mother tongue is Turkish or Kurdish, or the million Bosnians, Serbs and Croatians, cannot watch public (subsidised) TV programmes for children or for adults in their own language. Most of these approximately 8.5 million people, who have either been or are about to be naturalised, pay monthly TV and/or radio licence fees. Yet they rarely, if ever, become the subject of a broadcast or are even singled out as a target audience, nor are they employed as producers or anchors. There is, of course, government funding for the Sorbian-German theatre in Bautzen. Yet well-funded and established platforms for German-Turkish, German-Kurdish or German-Italian theatre, cinema or music performances are few and far between.

This poor record can be hardly compensated for by performances of operas by Mozart, Verdi or Puccini in their Italian original version, or by TV-specials on the Arte-Channel (a French-German public TV co-operation based in Strasbourg) showing films by local directors and in the original languages about Turkey, the Maghreb or Iran.

This is why so many immigrants from the Mediterranean region as well as their children and grandchildren watch evening shows broadcast by satellite from their home countries. The issues these programmes focus on interest them more than do German domestic politics, German talk shows or the kind of culture which appeals to Germans.

In matters of religion the situation is not much different. At present about 3 million Muslims live in Germany, many of whom have lived here for more than 40 years. Yet for them, or rather, for their children, hardly any state-approved religious education is provided at our schools, although Protestants, Catholics and Jews each have such programmes. Instead, we let various Islamic groups take care of religious education. Moreover, our universities choose not to train teachers of Islamic studies, although we complain bitterly about the influence of religious preachers, teachers and imams who are financed by Saudi Arabia, Turkey or non-governmental organisations.

Unlike in the 1960s, when Germany invited thousands of "guest workers" into the country, our attitude today is quite clear: those who come and want to stay should integrate. They should learn German and accept the basic tenets of German culture. The language, religion and culture of an immigrant's home country are seen exclusively as a private matter, or even as a hurdle to integration. They are tolerated, but, as a rule, they are viewed as contributing nothing to German culture and are thus considered unworthy of being preserved. This is largely the result of our "mythical goal" of an ethnically pure nation-state.

At the same time, we have established a hierarchy of national languages and cultures – we differentiate between languages which we consider useful, valuable or important and those that are not. This alone explains why in quite a few German schools classes are taught in English and French, while there are practically no schools where Turkish is part of the curriculum, let alone used as the teaching medium. Serbian, Kurdish or Albanian are never taught at schools here. Immigrants and their children – according to public opinion – are better off learning German. While justified in some respects, this requirement misses at least two points: in immigrant families, where parents often have a poor command of their own language, children have little chance to learn correct German. In addition, knowledge of foreign languages (whatever the language may be) is an important asset not just for the individual possessor, but also for Germany's socio-economic system.

We are not talking about replacing our current society with a multicultural mosaic that lacks a dominant lingua franca. The issue here, rather, is how to put an existing potential of cultural and language skills to better use. These skills, possessed by immigrants and their children, could improve Germany's competitive position abroad.

In the future, Germany will depend more than ever before on immigration. There are 82 million people living in Germany at present. This number will fall to about 59 million by the end of the first half of this century if no immigration takes place. The decline will involve mostly children, teenagers and people of employment age. That is why we need a controlled immigration process. This includes targeting groups of immigrants whose arrival would benefit us. We are going to have to compete with other industrialised nations for such "profitable" immigrants. Our success or failure in this competition will depend on factors which go beyond the opportunities provided by the local labour market and overall economic conditions. Such factors will include the degree of tolerance or intolerance shown to immigrants and their children born here and also the existence or absence of ethnic "communities", networks and ethnic infrastructures. Such structures, if present, provide immigrants with considerable support when they take their first steps in their new host country.

Germany is becoming more diverse. The presence of foreigners and naturalised Germans is a proof of that. Future immigrants will intensify this development, with new ethnic communities appearing alongside the existing ones. That is why now, more than ever, the majority and the minorities should think hard about their dealings with each other. It is not enough to call for mutual tolerance. Rather, the issue is to agree on the rules of the game and the players' rights and obligations.

Therefore it is not enough for the majority to set down what it expects from immigrants and naturalised citizens. We

188   should also be talking about what the minorities might expect from the majority.

Rainer Münz
Sociologist. Member of the Panel on Migration of the German government.

Born in 1954 in Basel, Switzerland. Studied sociology and philosophy at the University of Vienna. Received his Ph.D. in 1978. Lecturer and researcher at the Institute of Demography of the Austrian Academy of Sciences. Guest professor at Berkeley, Frankfurt (Main) and Zurich. Professor of Demographic Studies at the Humboldt University in Berlin since 1992.

Selected publications: *Migration in Europa 1945–2000. Aktuelle Trends, soziale Folgen, politische Reaktionen* (ed., 1996); *Zuwanderung nach Deutschland. Strukturen, Wirkungen, Perspektiven* (co-ed., 1997); *Migrants, Refugees and Foreign Policy. U.S. and German Policies Toward Countries of Origin* (co-ed., 1997); *Paths to Inclusion. The Integration of Immigrants in the United States and Germany* (ed., 1997); *Ost-West-Wanderung in Europa. Rückblick und Ausblick* (ed., 1998).

NIGEL BARLEY

THE BEGINNING OF THE END: AN EVENING WITH LILITH

Adam and Eve lived in the Garden of Eden where everything was just perfect. There was to be found all the rich diversity of Nature, yet everything lived without conflict or friction in a state of perfect tolerance. Everybody knows the story. It is a picture that has inspired utopias through the ages. But wait... before Eve there was, it seems, another wife, Lilith, who according to some sources, was just too noisy, too sexy and, instead of staying in the kitchen, ran away to become a demon. What was her view of Paradise? Well it seems she's emerged from retirement and is finally giving interviews. I went along to see her...

The lights in the Waldorf-Astoria were muted with pink bulbs chosen to be flattering. "Demons don't die, honey. But we do get old. Not as quick as you because we've partaken of the tree of life but still..." Her voice trailed off and hung in the air like the smell of the cigarette she was smoking.

Lilith was a woman in the full flower of her maturity, dark hair unfashionably long, kohled eyes, rich red mouth, body that New Yorkers call zoftig, full – almost pneumatic – plumped-like-a-cushion rather than just plump. The skin was olive with a sheen that promised musky exhalations and delicate palpation. She was the sort of woman who made you think not of roses and violets but big, heavy lilies, wet from their last spraying in a pricey florists.

"I'm not nocturnal but I sleep late, haven't gone out much the last few thousand years." She crossed her legs with a soft silken rustle that spoke louder than a big bass drum. "All that's just the constraint of etymology, the voice of the people." Lilith batted kohled lids tiredly. "In Hebrew my name's like the word for screech-owl, so all that vampire stuff got dumped on me. My real thing's storms, the blackness of storms, raging, swirling winds." Her teeth, small and sharp bit into her lower lip wetly. "Exciting," she whispered and shuddered, tossing her hair.

There was a pause as she sipped from her glass. It looked like some pale, expensive Scotch, clinking with ice. "Another," she ordered and pointed to the decanter on the table over by the wall. I took her glass and refilled it. With Lilith, it did not occur to you to take offence. It did not occur to her to invite you to join her.

"I don't normally give interviews," she said. "It's a capitalist press out there. My sister and I were from Assyria. They never liked us. Look at the way they wrote me up – really gets my goat." There was sharp East Coast bitterness in the voice behind the fashion model's assumed languor. Occasionally other accents and locutions drifted up like the ghostly tastes that flicker past when you slosh old red wine back and forth over your tongue. "Then there was the Whore of Babylon. I swear they modelled her on me and my sister – crucified us. I should have sued. Not like that poet Keats. He knew how to treat a Lamia." She sipped her drink and watched me with careful eyes over the rim.

"You want to know what really happened." It was not a question but a statement. "It was all hushed up. They kept it out of the papers – afraid of the scandal. What the hell. It's time I came clean. It's a scratch and sniff creation."

She sank back on the lush sofa and looked up at the ceiling, holding in a lungful of cigarette smoke.

"It's the oldest story in the world," she said exhaling curlicues. She blew more. "At least, it is now. Then it was the newest. People were tolerant in those days. Angels, demons, animals, it didn't much matter. Nobody minded. Biology was at a formative stage and, of course, religion hadn't been invented. It was one big party. Boy, then the lion really did lie down with the lamb. Some of those young bucks…" She looked briefly wistful and absurdly young. "In the Garden the sun shone all the time. We had night and day but no seasons. It was as if the two just switched back and forth. Always the same night. The same day. No thought for the morrow. Because there was no morrow, no insecurity. It was eternally today. Right here. Right now. There was a big high wall to keep anything nasty out. Anytime you wanted a drink you tapped into a wine palm. The fruit fell off the trees into your mouth. There was great grass. We were all vegetarians of course.

There was this accident. Nobody's fault. We said it was an act of God. He didn't like that. You see, He had this tree he was really gone on. The tree of knowledge. He was always at it – couldn't leave it alone – forever shovelling up dung with His divine hands and dumping it round the tree, watering it, polishing the leaves. It was nothing to look at, sort of skinny and grey with wild, nasty branches shooting out all over and poking people in the eye. And you know, it was weird – somehow never quite the same shape as the last time you looked at it. It always seemed as if the trunk would chicken out under the weight. And horrible-looking fruit like an elephant's scrotum. You getting all this, honey?"

I nodded, scribbling, anxious not to interrupt the flow.

"All this botany is redundant. The point is the boss, the CEO, God, he loved to see that thing grow. "Thus", he would intone, "knowledge increaseth daily upon the face of the Earth" and dumped more dung. It was a sort of divine transfer of technology programme, I think. All the fruit-eaters were totally banned from the tree. The fowl of the air couldn't nest in it, or squirrels make holes. Once He caught a deer peeing near it and went ape.

Anyway, this accident. Some of the early ungulates were horsing around, no monkey business or anything like that. They were simply exulting in the possession of hooves, as juveniles will, and playing catch-me-kiss-me round the tree. One barged into it and broke a whole branch off. "Well", I said, "there goes cost-benefit analysis". What the hell. It would probably grow back in a few thousand years.

Oh, we all stuck together of course, called up all the herbivores and termites to eat it up but – oh hostile fortune – He had to choose that moment to do His rounds and see the damn tree how it waxeth and instead found us all like a bunch of asses chewing away with our butts in the air.

So we got Adam. The idea was he was to be a sort of park keeper with dominion over the beasts of creation and spend his life serving that tree and picking up litter. But none of the animals had any respect for him. God treated him like he was dirt, always rabbiting on at him in his voice of thunder. It was Adam do this and Adam don't do that. And Adam was just divine – well no, not divine – earthy. He smelled of sweat. He was real cute even if he didn't have a tail."

"A tail?" I hadn't meant to interrupt.

She held out the glass for a refill. I laid down pen and paper and went over to the decanter to pour.

"Sure, a tail. Not having a tail is an aesthetic disaster. Think of all the great etiquette and gestures you can work out with tails, when to drape it over your knee while sitting and when not. When to wag it in joy and twitch it in smouldering rage. The marvellous insult of slapping some bastard across the face with your tail. The sexual potential…."

She sighed, rested her head on her arm and looked along it at me. I handed her the glass and she flashed me a smile hot enough to start a bushfire.

"You know, there's something of the old Adam in you. He had better pecs of course but then every day this mortal

world declineth and fadeth away and I suppose you are related – albeit distantly."

Not bothering to blush, I sat down and picked up the paper and pen as a sign she should start again.

"There was no such thing as marriage in those days – we
had what you might term a free-form union, free as birds. I
was Adam's madam. He was a new model and everyone was
keen to try him out. But I . . .", her bosom swelled like a battle standard, ". . . was first. Cain and Abel were both mine by
him. I know . . .", she shot me a scalding look, ". . . it doesn't
say that in the Bible but they wrote me out of the main story.
And I did most of the naming of things, not Adam. Adam
was a pussy cat but he couldn't tell shit from chihuahua. That
bit of the tree of knowledge I ate had to go somewhere."

She mashed out the end of her cigarette and immediately lit
another Camel – no business about holding it out to me for a
light.

"Then God had one of His bouts of segregationism, con-
formism, political correctness, because he was still miffed
about the damned tree. He split up some really happy couples –
and trios come to that. "Abominations" was the new buzz-
word. Like could only go with like. "Unclean" was another.
"Unclean" builds morality into nature. Complain and you
were out of the Garden. Tolerance has no natural bounds – this
far and no further – but once you classify, you've got rules and
people who don't conform are acting against nature. My whole
life has been one long act against nature."

She sighed huskily, stubbed, relit. "Have you ever thought
how weird God is, no physical functions, nothing below the
waist? It's the explanation for just about everything in this
world. He drifts . . . Nothing to keep his feet on the ground. I
had to put Cain and Abel up for adoption but Adam got custody. No one knew about alimony. There were no lawyers –
not yet. And God made that foxy little bitch Eve. She was a
genetic clone, you know? God was so obsessed with trees,
He even made the first woman by taking a cutting. She was

identical to Adam in every way except for the obvious. Adam used to say that having sex with her was like masturbation looking in a mirror. And that kid of theirs, Seth. He was just the same, the great dumb ox. The whole bunch of them only had one face between them."

"The apple", I said. "That was you too wasn't it?"

She reached behind her neck and batted out the long hair that rested against it with the back of her hand, a great aromatic streamer.

"Yes. That was me. I had this friend, Nat. He was a serpent, a bit of a wolf, cool dude, attractively sinister. Funny little legs like a dachshund but beautiful markings, lovely mover. He was a great dancer till he lost the legs. He helped me. He got close to Eve, jollied her along, spoke with forked tongue, sold her a pup I suppose – that kind of thing anyway. She could tell Adam was bored to death with her. But a hard man is good to find. Nat suggested the road to a man's basic instincts was straight down the oesophagus. "Give him something new to eat", he said. "Some new fruit. You'll be the apple of his eye." None of us had cooking then. That was invented by my boys much later. If we had, she could have done him spaghetti bolognese and the whole history of the world might have been different.

Well, you know what happened. She slipped him the scrotum fruit. God went through the roof. Seems she'd knocked out most of jurisprudence with a couple of bites. Oh yes. It wasn't an apple. That's just more etymology and PR cockup. In the Latin translation malum means both *apple* and *evil*. Oh yes, another thing, it tasted like death – made Adam sick as a parrot for days. Who would've guessed the fruit of the tree of knowledge would be poisonous?

Nat and I got canned. The Garden was sold off for redevelopment. My son Cain went into real estate much later and made a killing. Eve thought she'd done really well having invented fashion. All she'd really invented was weekly washing. Poor Adam! The poor putz had been framed. He stood by her, lost his job and ended up a common labourer, a dog's life. Eve got wilder and wilder, downhill all the way. God could be so judgmental and so catty so He cut Adam down in his prime, only 930 years old. What the Hell, maybe it wasn't so bad. You could say Adam got life with Eve, commuted to death on appeal. As an afterthought He gave us disease. The first thing I got after leaving the Garden was a boil on the tush."

"What did you do? Where did you go?"

"Here, there, around. You rend your raiment, gnash your teeth but life goes on. Look here." She leaned forward and displayed an expanse of cleavage. Unwittingly literal, I looked there.

"We were supposed to drop everything and get married – actually in the reverse order, shape up. I wasn't ready for any commitment, not yet, but I'm a woman. I have needs." She set her face in defiance. "Nocturnal visitations was my bag. A lot of us independent lady demons did that. We'd beguile men in the middle of the night in their sleep and stir them up a little. Don't say we didn't get around to you."

Now I blushed. She laughed. "I told you you looked familiar. It was fun. It did no harm. Mortals weren't even called to book for it, a moral freebie like trading stamps. We kept most of the early hermits from going over the edge, a sort of safety valve, a positive social function. Recently, I've taken up charity work. Read the Rabbinical fathers. I look after children born out of wedlock. Someone has to."

"Cain and Abel", I urged gently. "What happened?"

She dug in a snakeskin handbag that matched her shoes – Nat? I wondered – and dabbed at her eyes with a delicate handkerchief, blearing through a veil of tears but careful not to let emotion smear the makeup. Then she kicked off the shoes and tucked her legs up under her backside with a flash of golden calves.

"In those days we were all much closer to the animals. Like I say, we sort of overlapped – in every sense. Single births were unknown till that cow Eve. Both Cain and Abel had twin sisters. One was beautiful. The other was a real dog. Who else were they supposed to marry? So the boys fell out over who did what with which and to whom. Everyone had the same problem in those days. Look at Abraham. Every time he went somewhere he passed his wife Sarah off as his sister and hired her out for private functions. Funny thing is she was his sister – same father, different mother. And there were all those slapstick routines in the Old Testament, wives sending in veiled servant girls to sleep with their husbands, Noah and his own daughters, Jacob putting on furry gloves to pretend he was his brother, ugly Leah sliding into the nuptial chamber instead of luscious Rebecca, the angels and the gay community at Sodom. Trapdoors, disguises, the dropping of drawers, ooh la la! All that stuff was a gas. Only later did they try to pretend it was all serious.

The trouble between my two boys? I blame the stepmother. *When Adam delved and Eve span*, you know the poem? Don't make me laugh. That Jewish Mesopotamian Princess sat around all day and brought the art of nailcare to unprecedented levels of development. She made Abel a real Moma's boy. He was the first shepherd, but I suppose you know that. You live with sheep, you get to think like them – woolly. Cain went off and worked on agrarian innovation projects. He thought God would like that. How was he to know God had changed, turned funny over all plants after the Garden, gone meat-eating, liking human flesh? And anyway, God was after a world view for Man, a coordinated mission statement. You want some neat judgmental rituals to bring together authority structures, dietary regulations, incest rules, bodily pollutions and abominations – go for animal schemata. Gets disapproval and outrage into the world, the engine that drives progress along. Plant metaphors are hopeless. Too forgiving – all that endless recycling and renewal, dung-to-fertiliser, evil-to-good stuff, leads to tolerance. The world had to move on. So shepherd Abel became His pet and Cain the black sheep."

She broke off and yawned. The cigarette was finished, the drink reduced to emaciated slivers of ice. "Enough for to-day." There was something bright and dangerous in her look as she turned it full blast on me, a storm warning. Her teeth looked suddenly longer and sharper. Her rump shifted itchily on the sofa, like a cat rubbing itself against a fridge. It was time to go.

"You want to fool around a little, honey? One for the memoirs?"

It was an uncomfortable moment. "I really am most fright-fully honoured but – well – I don't think we're closely enough related for that."

She laughed. It was a good laugh, bold, brassy and service-able like an old-fashioned doorknocker. "Honey", she shot me a look that sizzled, "now you be sure and give my love to your sister."

Nigel Barley
Assistant Keeper, Department of Ethnography, British Museum.

Born in 1947 in Kingston, United Kingdom. Read Modern Languages and Ethnology at Cambridge and Oxford. Lecturer in Social Anthropology at University College London 1975–77, joined the British Museum in 1980.

Selected publications: *Symbolic Structures of the Dowayos* (1983); *The Innocent Anthropologist* (1983); *A Plague of Caterpillars* (1986); *Native Land* (1989); *The Coast* (1990); *The Duke of Puddle Dock* (1993); *Dancing on the Grave* (1995); *White Rajah* (2001).

At any rate,
I'd rather be a square something
than a round nothing.

FRIEDRICH HEBBEL

Peter Blake (*1932), G for Girl (Alphabet Series), undated

THE PILLARS OF TOLERANCE:
FAITH AND RELIGION

HANS KÜNG

MANY FAITHS – ONE TOLERANCE

These days you hear everywhere that politics – especially global politics – have changed forever since the September 11 terrorist attacks in the United States. Yet this is only partly true. Well before these tragic events, some experienced observers had already seen change coming and raised their voices in alarm. What happened that day largely confirmed the experts' premonitions. Now they are saying – and I agree with them – that the future of the human race and the future of religious faiths will depend to a great extent on whether or not religion can become a source of freedom, mutual understanding and reconciliation. Religions that lead to war, intolerance, fanaticism and fundamentalism push mankind to the brink of self-destruction. The human race will find peace only if people of all faiths commit themselves to actively promoting peace and mutual understanding.

NO GLOBAL POLITICS WITHOUT GLOBAL ETHOS

Despite the horrors of the 20th century, "a hesitant historical progress nevertheless appears to be taking place," says Dieter Senghaas, a famous Bremen-based political scientist and peace researcher in his critical essay on "Political Conditions for a Global Ethos".[1] The *dominant political value systems of the last century are obviously bankrupt:*

- *Imperialism* disappeared after the last colonies fell.
- *Racism* as a consistent policy of racial discrimination is no longer explicitly practiced by any state since the end of apartheid in South Africa.
- *Nationalism* has become a taboo word in western Europe where it originated and has been replaced by "European integration", with economic competition taking the place of military confrontation.

Should, perhaps, Samuel Huntington's "clash of civilisations," rather than these outdated ideologies, become the dominant political theory? Senghaas believes it is highly unlikely to happen, because these civilisations (Islam, Confucianism, etc) are not global players: they are far from being homogeneous and are fraught with internal strife. They neither control nor dominate any nation states. His statement supports my view that Huntington's theory of a "clash of civilisations" is *a poor compass* for future world politics. Huntington's theory:

- lacks any basis and is empirically unfounded;
- calls for an old "block model": the West against Islam, the West against the Confucian civilisation of China;
- ignores the overlapping of values and common ground between cultures.

But Senghaas also points out that a discussion of *global ethos* remains important, because it makes abundantly clear "how introspective the world is becoming". Cross-cultural ethical values – such as "golden rules" – play an important role in this process. Even more vital is "a slow and controversial process of agreeing on such concepts". Discarding worn-out ideologies, this process would jolt mankind's self-awareness.

While international conferences provide an important, albeit insufficiently used platform for global politics, the Global Ethos Project has been "initiated by a society of citizens; many more such projects should exist in the future – and indeed they will". Until now, far too few artists and scientists have taken part in this process; however, this situation seems to be changing gradually. "In retrospect, the Global Ethos Project will be seen as an innovative programme and will definitely play a more prominent role."

Senghaas is right in saying the Global Ethos Project cannot exist in a vacuum. Instead, it must be incorporated into a web of individual societies, encompass regional cooperation and reach all the way to the level of international systems. From this perspective, the Global Ethos Project must be seen as an integral part of an *entire network of achievements of civilisation* that make peaceful coexistence possible via a constructive handling of conflicts. At least six achievements with a global reach stand out (Senghaas calls them "the civilization hexagon"): state monopoly on the use of force, the rule of law, the defusing of conflict situations and crowd control, democratic participation of new social classes, fair allocation of social benefits, and the development of a culture of constructive conflict resolution.

Again, I can only agree with Senghaas that such achievements were secured in Europe *in the face of European tradition*, even in conflict with it. At the same time I must admit that, in a sense, these achievements were made at least partially *because of European tradition!*

Why is this so? The "culturally essential" parameter of such a collective learning process (its inherence in Western culture) is far less important than its "historico-cultural" aspects. Although political *constraints* have hampered this process, *positive stimuli* from European cultural traditions have advanced it. After all, how could Europe have arrived at the present state of civilisation without the momentum created by Socrates, Plato and Aristotle, by Augustine and

206 Thomas, by Luther, Calvin, Erasmus and Comenius, by Vittoria, Suarez, and Las Casas? How could the "ethos of the modern democratic constitutional state" have developed if Stoicism, Scholasticism, the Reformation, Humanism and the early Enlightenment had not sensitised society to the rules of human conduct, moderation, tolerance, willingness to compromise and fairness? These ideologies must be viewed as broad trends of tradition, with negative aspects often mixed in, rather than isolated episodes.

It is important to differentiate between positive and negative elements in European tradition. *First of all*, only its ambivalent "pre-history" can explain why such civilisation achievements took place exclusively in Europe, rather than in India, China or Japan. *Secondly*, only from this perspective can we explain why other cultural regions outside Europe don't have *"to replicate in principle"* such achievements but have been able to draw on their own traditions in the civilisation process. No-one is expecting non-European nations to slavishly imitate western European cultural canons; yet it would be equally unwelcome if they tried to shelter their reactionary traditions or embrace the know-how of the West while rejecting its intellectual legacy. The adoption of European innovations by non-European nations is unavoidable, but because of their traditions it would have a different and unpredictable effect. What will emerge in these nations will have new features, partly contrary to their traditions and partly stemming from them, so that while old ashes remain well-protected, the fire will be passed on.

Efforts to shape a global ethos are being undertaken against the background of civilisation-forming trends, structures, institutions and mindsets. Such efforts are focusing on more than mere compatibility of basic values vital for the development of society, such as common norms, standards, views and virtues. They can also help "foster cross-border communication and transactions". "Responsiveness", seen by Senghaas as a key characteristic, plays a very special role in these processes. And while Confucius called such "reciprocity" ("shu") a virtue, the golden rule said it best: "Do unto others as you would have them do unto you." Yet, despite Rabbi Hillel's preachings and the Sermon on the Mount extolling this concept, it is this rule that is most seriously violated by religions.

RELIGIONS IN WORLD CONFLICTS

The Tübingen-based political scientists Volker Rittberger and Andreas Hasenclever have documented the ambivalence of religions towards political conflicts in our eventful times and at the same time offered a critical analysis in an informative and lucid essay.[2] They back their criticism of Huntington's clash theory with statistics on the number of *wars* within the cultural circles identified by Huntington (intra-civilisational wars in Somalia, Algeria, Egypt, Ruanda, Sudan, Afghanistan and in South America) and by citing numerous alliances between people from different cultures (inter-civilisational alliances between United States and Japan, South Korea, Taiwan, as well as U.S. activities in Yemen, Sudan and in the Gulf War).

At the same time, these experts show that *religious conflicts* are above all based on *modernisation conflicts*: ambitious elites exploit traditional religious beliefs in order to foster public protest. In other words, fundamentalist movements are reactions to governments' failure to achieve modernisation and overcome developmental crises: political radicalisation of religion regularly follows economic and social impoverishment. I do not know if this is always the case. Certainly many militant clashes are proxies for underlying conflicts over fair distribution of power and social benefits, while religious and cultural aspects are less important. "So 'the clash of cultures' could only be really taking place in crisis-shaken societies, where strife over economic, social and power-distribution issues could become quite disruptive."

Rittberger and Hasenclever believe that while religion can *intensify conflicts*, it can also help *de-escalate* them. This is especially true in basically unavoidable conflicts, where religion can help avoid a violent outburst and reach a peaceful solution. In this respect, I find their current political analysis of the issue particularly enlightening. According to these analysts, two factors determine whether or not decision-makers would choose violence as a strategy. One factor is their ability *to mobilise their followers*. Value conflicts that pose an existential threat for the group and thus make compromises barely possible are substantially more prone to cause violence than more mundane interest conflicts. The greater the willingness to bring sacrifices on the part of the followers, and the less trust there is between the conflicting parties, the more feasible it is that the conflict will end in violence. At the same time, the probability of applying violence as a strategy increases *with the level of support provided by society*: the chances for each conflicting party to win depend largely on the degree of popular support it has.

In any case, the combination of the elites' political goals and religious convictions can provide a "highly explosive mix." Through the use of religious symbols, one's own claims and those made by others are increased, the willingness to bring sacrifices rises, and the trust between the conflicting parties is destroyed. How can the danger of escalation be minimised under these circumstances? What *opposing strategies* are possible?

- One basic strategy would be to promote *development and democratisation*, which improve the economic and social situation in the societies involved. Such a strategy, however, would require a government capable of implementing it – and this is seldom the case in the crisis-shaken countries of the southern hemisphere.
- Current peace and conflict researchers are quite sceptical about *intimidation* and *oppression strategies*, whose success in all but a few cases has been rather questionable, as inter-

national experience in countries from Algeria to East
Timor has shown.

- Peace researchers attach increasing importance to *the dialogue strategy.* Such dialogue tries to strengthen moderates
rather than militant fundamentalists, since the former are
more apt to hold that the use of force in political disputes
is inappropriate and immoral and therefore would refuse to
support an armed fight.

The goal of dialogue strategy is to influence the moral attitudes of the conflicting parties in order to win the proverbial "battle for the mind" by providing the moderates with
better arguments. Here the two Tübingen political scientists, completely in accord with the Global Ethos Project,
see "the chance for major religious faiths to promote
peace." They say that much would be won "if the representatives of the world religions would stop legitimising
wars and begin to preach their religious vision of peace and
the principle that members of other religions must be protected". Since religious thinking remains highly heterogeneous and certain religious persuasions traditionally, at
least to some degree, propagate violence, it is necessary to
emphasise interpretations that hold violence and faith to be
incompatible, that demand sacrifices for peace, and that
require respect for those of other beliefs.

Rittberger and Hasenclever point to *the power of religion to
promote peace* in the *protest movements* that seek radical political reforms and at the same time oblige their members to
observe strictly non-violent behaviour (Gandhi, Martin
Luther King, Dalai Lama, South African Church Council)
and in the religious communities that provide *mediation* in
political conflicts (Central America).

The researchers insist that if religious communities could
"agree on common behaviour rules" and then also "practice"
them, this would be a decisive factor in the current situation.
This is how they interpret the declarations by the World

Religion Conference for Peace in 1970 and above all the Declaration of the Parliament of World Religions in Chicago in 1993.

THE GLOBAL ETHOS PROJECT

In "practical" political science, but also in world politics itself, the problems of *global ethical responsibility* are moving into the focus of public attention. When I published the book "Global Ethos Project" ("Projekt Welt Ethos") in 1990, I had difficulty finding any documents published by world organisations on global ethics. But just three years after "Global Ethos Project" was published, *the Declaration of the Parliament of World Religions on Global Ethos* (1993) came out, a challenging undertaking which I had the honour to prepare. Six years later, when I developed what I hope is a realistic, forward-looking synopsis under the title "Global Ethos for Global Politics and Economy", further important international documents were published by the United Nations Commission for World Order Politics, by the World Commission for Culture and Development, and by the InterAction Council of former national and government leaders.

It is gratifying to know that by now a number of experienced and quite realistic statesmen, such as the members of the InterAction Council, have adopted two very fundamental principles as the basis for the world ethos: "Every person should be treated humanely", and the already-mentioned golden rule: "Do unto others as you would have them do unto you." These norms are valid for all areas of life, not only for individuals, but also for families and communities, for peoples, nations and religions.

Both declarations have received full backing from an extensive report by the United Nations, "Crossing the Divide: Dialogue among Civilisations". A group of high-ranking public figures chosen by the Secretary-General Kofi Annan put together this report for the "2001: International Year of Dialogues between Cultures" and presented it to the United Nations General Assembly for discussion. It contains the following topics: dialogue between civilisations, globalisation, a new paradigm of international relationships, and global ethos.[5]

The ethical basis for the Chicago Declaration is extremely elemental although not necessarily obvious: it is humanity in the true sense, as derived from humaneness. The Chicago Declaration says: "As in the past, people continue to be treated in an inhumane fashion everywhere in the world. They are being robbed of their chances in life and their freedom, their human rights are being ignored, their human dignity disregarded. But power is not the same as justice! In view of such inhumane treatment, our religious and ethical convictions demand that *every human being should be treated humanely.* This means that every person, regardless of age, sex, race, skin colour, physical or mental abilities, language, religion, political views, national or social origin possesses an inalienable and sacrosanct dignity."

It is not just the individual who needs a set of moral rules; society needs *a social ethos.* The morality of *institutions* depends on the *personal integrity* of their employees. Thus it is vital that systems and institutions work on reinforcing these concepts in people's minds. *Four such final commandments,* inherent in all religious and ethical traditions of mankind, have found their way into both Global Ethos documents:

- The obligation of a society to promote a culture of non-violence and respect for all life. Worship life! Particularly at a time when children murder other children, we should reinforce the ancient commandment: "Thou shall not kill!"
- The obligation of a society to promote a culture of solidarity and a just economic order, particularly in a period of globalisation. Be fair and just! Hence the ancient commandment: "Thou shall not steal!"

212

- The obligation of a society to promote cultural tolerance and a life of veracity. Speak and act truthfully! In view of so many political and media scandals, the reinforcement of the ancient commandment: "Thou shall not lie!"
- The obligation of a society to promote cultural equality and the partnership of husband and wife. Respect and love one another! Especially in our times of unprecedented freedom from taboos, the ancient commandment rings true: "Thou shall not misuse sex!"

Of course, these are just words, so it is up to people, especially those in positions of authority, to put these principles into effect. But I am convinced more than ever that without *the will to do the ethical thing*, without a moral centrifugal force, without moral energy, the *key problems of the 21st century cannot be tackled, much less solved.* September 11 demonstrated to those who had not taken these problems seriously where religious intolerance can lead. Today, many are changing their minds as they are beginning to see that religious faiths can reach into their own resources to overcome a tradition of intolerance and even go beyond sheer "tolerance". Today it is necessary to achieve solidarity among the people of different cultures and religions as well as cooperation on both the local level (in numerous multicultural and multi-religious cities), and on the global level – under the banners of global communications, global economy, global ecology, and global politics.

NOTES

1 Cf. D. Senghaas, "Politische Rahmenbedingungen für ein Weltethos", in: H. Küng, K.-J. Kuschel, *Wissenschaft und Weltethos*, München 1998, p. 141.

2 Cf. V. Rittberger, A. Hasenclever, "Religionen in Konflikten", in: H. Küng, K.-J. Kuschel, *Wissenschaft und Weltethos*, pp. 161-200.

3 Cf. H. Küng, K.-J. Kuschel (eds.), *Erklärung zum Weltethos. Die Deklaration des Parlamentes der Weltreligionen*, München 1993, p. 26.
4 Cf. H. Küng, *Weltethos für Weltpolitik und Weltwirtschaft*, München 1997
5 Cf. United Nations, *Crossing the Divide: Dialogue among Civilizations*, New York 2001; see: www.un.org/dialogue

Hans Küng

Theologian. Founder of "The Foundation Global Ethos for Intercultural and Interreligious Research, Education, Experience".

Born in 1928 in Sursee, Switzerland. Studied Philosophy and Theology. Ordained as a priest. Became official theological advisor (peritus) to the Second Vatican Council, appointed by Pope John XXIII. Full Professor of Dogmatic and Ecumenical Theology in Tübingen 1960; since 1980 under direct responsibility of the University President and Senate.

Selected Publications: *Christianity: Essence, History and Future* (1996); *The Incarnation of God* (2000); *The Catholic Church: A short history* (2001); *Tracing the Way* (2001); *Erklärung zum Weltethos. Die Deklaration des Parlaments der Weltreligionen* (co-authored in 1993); *Christ sein* (1993); *Existiert Gott?* (1995); *Weltethos für Weltpolitik und Weltwirtschaft* (1997); *Brücken in die Zukunft. Ein Manifest für den Dialog der Kulturen* (co-authored in 2001).

CHRISTOPH SCHWÖBEL

THE ECUMENICAL CONTRIBUTION

The history of tolerance is the history of religious freedom. The most radical challenge to a person's identity is the confrontation with convictions of alien faiths that question the very foundation on which that identity is built. The issue of tolerance therefore presents itself in its most extreme form when it concerns the tolerance of alien religious convictions and alien religious communities.

Today we encounter the diversity of orientations and life styles in all spheres of social life. Cultural, ideological and religious diversity is no longer primarily found outside the confines of our own society, but inside its boundaries in concrete situations of our everyday lives. The stranger has become a neighbour. A consensus on fundamental values can no longer be presumed; on the contrary, all questions of orientation have to be renegotiated in all areas of life.

In Europe, this situation is the result of a long history of pluralisation that began with the Reformation. In the Reformation, the single all-encompassing Christian church was replaced by two churches, or two religions, as people described them in the 16th century. The impetus of this pluralisation process continued to be felt in the Protestant churches, which had emerged as a plurality at the very outset and continued to expand through schisms and unions. The experience of religious wars demonstrated the destructive potential of religion when it was instrumentalised for national territorial ends. It also made the issue of tolerance a matter of life and death not only for the co-existence of societies with different religious beliefs, but also for co-existence within confessionally pluralistic societies. The notions of tolerance that developed against the background of this experience are founded upon a fundamental consensus of religious and ethical beliefs that tie society together. On the basis of this underlying consensus, religious dissent can be tolerated as long as it is confined to the sphere of private religious practice and does not threaten the basis of life within society. The separation of general fundamental principles, which describe the social consensus, and specific religious beliefs eventually led to a situation in which the foundations of secular life were no longer determined by religion after the kind of reason, engendered by the Enlightenment became the basis for the general consensus. The separation of church and state, already inchoate in this difference, therefore inaugurated the ideological neutrality of the state and the privatisation of religion.

The history of the concept of tolerance in different religions can thus contribute to uncovering not only the religious obstacles to tolerance, but also its religious roots. This history is rather ambivalent because all religions that emerged within the contexts of established religious traditions were initially forced to promote their own religious identity before being confronted with the question of whether and how they should show tolerance towards other religious orientations – after they in turn had asserted themselves as dominant religious traditions. The concept of tolerance in the modern age was formulated within a critique of the claims of religious tradition. The problematical nature of its history can be seen in the fact that the demand for tolerance appears to involve a relativisation of religious truth that weakens religious identity. And precisely this weakening of religious identity in turn transforms a fundamentalist affirmation of religion into intolerance against all other religious and ideological orientations. This dilemma, in which the demand for tolerance leads to intolerance, can only be avoided if tolerance can be based on religious truth itself, on the heart of religious identity. Are there religious roots of tolerance, foundations of tolerance that are based on religious identity and hence do not appear to challenge its validity?

Within the framework of Christian theology, a foundation of this kind can spring from the character of Christian faith. In the Christian understanding, faith is not a human accomplishment, but a contingently bestowed certainty about the truth of Christ's message. This certainty cannot be created, either by the believer himself or by anyone else. It must be freely revealed to the individual. Faith is freely given, not made. In the Christian view, this concept of how religious certainty comes about applies not only to Christians, but to all mankind, and it applies not only to the constitution of certainty in faith but to all certainties. This forms the foundation for the concept of freedom of conscience that emerged during the Reformation as part of the protest against the demands of ecclesiastical and secular rulers to tie conscience to existing teachings. From the perspective of the Christian faith, the recognition of the constitution of one's own certainty in faith leads to the recognition of the freedom of conscience as a result of the transcendental nature of conscience formation, which is the basis for tolerance of other religious faiths. In the view of the Christian faith, the truth of the foundation of faith in the transcendental nature of God's self-revelation implies that it applies to all mankind and to all certainties. Tolerance should therefore be shown towards other faiths because according to the witness of adherents to other religions these are also not the product of human endeavour for knowledge, but of a transcendental revelation experience.

The foundation of tolerance in the recognition of the constitution of one's own certainty in faith, i.e. on the basis of one's own religious identity, is radically different from the relativistic levelling of all religious truths.

Relativism proves an erroneous path to tolerance because at best it only concedes religious truth a partial understanding of the truth. Accordingly, tolerance is then based on the weakness of its understanding, the imperfection of its knowledge of truth. At the same time, however, relativism proves itself incapable of tolerance, because it lays claim to the absolute validity of its own dogma, "All truths are relative", while not tolerating a negation of the relativist tenet. Relativism claims exclusive legitimacy for its own position, while denying this to any other position: a classic attitude of intolerance. Tolerance is only possible as the active toleration of another truth, as the acceptance of someone else's right to uphold their certainties, when it is also based on certainty. The toleration of another faith is only possible as tolerance based on faith. This also reveals the reciprocity of tolerance, in which showing tolerance becomes the basis of stable relations between different convictions. Only if we show tolerance towards the convictions of others can we expect others to tolerate our convictions. While forced tolerance leads to intolerance, tolerance freely shown towards others contains an invitation to others to show tolerance in return.

This foundation of tolerance on the constitution of one's own certainty in faith – in Christian theological terms: on the experience of the freely given gift of faith, on the freedom of conscience of personal conviction, which can only be denied in the face of others' convictions at the cost of calling into question one's own convictions – also entails a clear realisation of the limits of tolerance. No attempt to interfere with the freedom of conscience can be tolerated, regardless whether this involves its repudiation or the attempt to actively form belief. The common denominator of all totalitarian ideologies is the fact that they seek not only to create certainties, but also to limit the validity of freedom of conscience based on the certainty of conviction.

We thus have a foundation for tolerance based on the recognition of the constitution of our own certainty in faith that makes it possible to show tolerance on the basis of faith. Is it, however, an abstract ideal type that must founder on the harsh realities of historical and social life and break down in the face of the reality of religious intolerance? At first glance, the resignative cynicism of intolerance towards the attempt to base tolerance on religious identity appears well-founded. Other experiences also exist, however, that suggest the chances of tolerance should not be nullified too soon. If one looks back at modern European history, which is characterised by bloody religious wars between different Christian religious communities, ecumenical understanding between the Christian churches in the 20th century represents a perhaps modest, but genuine advance in religious tolerance. Motivated by the experience of two world wars in which Christians fought on both sides, the ecumenical movement has opened opportunities for understanding and mutual tolerance among Christian churches that give rise to considerable grounds for hope after the long history of religious wars and violent inter-Christian conflicts.

Moreover, acknowledgment of the Christian churches' failure in the face of the Holocaust led to the recognition of a common responsibility on the part of the community of Christian churches to work together towards a just peace based on tolerance and recognition. Advances in ecumenical understanding make the continuing conflicts between Christian groups and the enduring threat to justice and peace posed by the confrontation of denominations, religions and ethnic groups especially painful. This experience does not invalidate the goal of a greater ecumenical understanding and ecumenical responsibility in the efforts for a just peace, it makes it even more pressing. In its modest results, ecumenical understanding represents a counter-model to the relativistic levelling of religious truth as the prerequisite for tolerance. Ecumenical understanding bases tolerance and mutual recognition on the reconciled difference of truth-convictions. Religious identity can therefore be understood as the condition for tolerance, and freely given tolerance as the prerequisite for the preservation of religious identity. Conclusions cannot be made in advance about the extent to which this model, which has proven itself in achieving understanding between Christian churches, can also be applied to increase understanding between different religions. At least, it would seem an alternative to the attempt to pacify religions by relativising their claims to truth – an attempt which has mainly created new intolerance. Against this background, the ecumenical understanding between churches as to their common responsibility represents a modest, but realistic contribution by Christian churches towards assuaging the clash of cultures and a small, but real step towards a community of dialogic difference.

Christoph Schwöbel
Theologian. Professor of Systematic Theology (Dogmatics and Ecumenical Theology) and Director of the Ecumenical Institute at Heidelberg University.

Born in 1955 in Frankfurt am Main, Germany. Studied evangelical theology in Bethel und Marburg. Received Ph.D. in Theology in 1978 in Marburg. Taught at Marburg University in 1981–1986. Director of the Research Institute for Systematic Theology, King's College, London University in 1986–1993. Professor for Systematic Theology at Kiel University in 1993–1999.

Selected publications: *God: Action and Revelation* (1991); *Trinitarian Theology Today. Essays on Divine Being and Act* (Ed., 1995)

DAN DINER

FROM DOCTRINE TO CONFESSION

The concept of tolerance is closely associated with the name
John Locke. The English philosopher stands for a tradition of
political tolerance that contributes to the pragmatic resolving
of conflicts. In Amsterdam, during the winter of 1685/86,
Locke wrote *A Letter Concerning Toleration* as a reaction to
the danger that had existed in England since 1679 of a curtail-
ment of religious freedom. Appearing quite some time after it
was written, the treatise, which did not refer to the concrete
historical circumstances that had inspired it, was a plea for the
separation of church and state, for the liberation of conscience from the control of ecclesiastical authorities as well as
for the limiting of state power to the guaranteeing of security
and property. Although Locke's letter on toleration was triggered by the current political situation, its main thrust went
far beyond that. In retrospect, it can certainly be seen as a
recommendation for secularisation – a further step towards
the transformation of the pre-modern structure of an all-em-
bracing religion into a denomination, an inner faith, which, in
effect, means the privatisation of religion.

With his plea for tolerance on the part of church and state
authorities of the transformation from a religion bound up
with the body politic to an individual faith, Locke goes

further than Thomas Hobbes. In *Leviathan*, by constantly repeating the emblematic formula "that Jesus is the Christ", Hobbes tries to attribute the neutralisation of the religious civil war by the all-powerful state to the common Christian heritage shared by all religious parties concerned. Locke's notion of a freedom of conscience beyond the grip of church and state goes far beyond that; it is more universal, since it promises religious freedom to non-Christians as well. Admittedly, atheists are excluded from toleration, mainly because for Locke, lack of faith was tantamount to the denial of all human obligations. A person who has rejected God and who therefore has no fear of eternal (as opposed to mere secular) punishment and no expectation of everlasting reward beyond worldly happiness is not capable of taking an oath. He cannot enter into contracts or be protected by law – he is simply outside of the law. In this respect, the atheist is regarded as a nihilist who rejects the very social order from which he himself must be expelled. Note that such an absolute exclusion from civil society casts an extremely interesting light on Locke's proverbial contractualism: without belief in a transcendent sphere and in divine might, contractual capability and its accompanying basic rule of *pacta sunt servanda* (contracts must be observed) are reduced to mere phrases. It is only through belief in God that contracted civil obligations can be met. Thus, even in the secular domain, belief in God takes on the importance of a last instance. Indeed – In God We Trust.

Religious belief is increasingly shifting to the private domain through secularisation. This benefits the internal peace of a society insofar as all previous religious discord is neutralised when religion moves from the political to the private sphere of the individual. The separation of the public and the private is significant for the emergence of modernity. In order to keep the public domain open to everybody, it has to be protected from eccentric beliefs that might shake society to its foundations. Locke cites the example of the Quakers, who are required by custom not to doff their hats in public. Their

222 unconventional behaviour introduces a distinguishing feature of a political nature into the public sphere. Such a feature fosters the creation of an arbitrary power that considers itself to be independent of state authority. According to Locke, it is not the mere displaying of "hats and turbans" that threatens law and order, but the oppositional and subversive attitude that this behaviour expresses – an attitude that has nothing to do with the individual expression of opinion or worship of God. Locke says that such provocative behaviour obviously signifies a desire to replace the existing public order with another, and he feels strongly that such a desire must be denied. Moreover, it should be opposed by sanctions, in other words: by means of intolerance. He claims that a wise government will know how to decide in each case whether or when such a threatening situation can be deemed to exist. If, then, it permits the public display of emblems which indicate a group affiliation, then it is letting it be understood that there is no danger to law and order. In accepting this breach of the rules, its action can be considered as tolerant. If, on the other hand, it sees law and order as endangered, then the authorities can consider measures that will turn their previously tolerant reaction into an intolerant one. It is this perception of the limits as to what is and what is not recognised as permissible that reflects the pragmatic core of Locke's concept of tolerance. Tolerance à la Locke, just like so many other notions as to the sense and purpose of tolerance, has a negative connotation. After all, tolerance represents the readiness to put up with things that could be prevented by an existing authority – but are not.

The Lockean concept of tolerance must be considered against the background of the process of secularisation, which was mainly relevant for the Christian denominations of the early modern period. The more the public sphere of the Christian state was able to free itself of elements of that faith and its denominations, the more open and universal it became. This applied in Europe to those countries where the emancipation of the Jews was taking place and also to successive waves of laicisation. The state shed its Christian character as the Christian religion for its part became a matter of personal belief, i.e. retreated into the private sphere. It was not until religion was privatised that people of different religious affiliations were able to share the public sphere as a common domain, which essentially meant that the originally external validity of required expressions of affiliation was being neutralised. Indeed, it was the shifting of religion to the personal level that made society "tolerant" the way Locke understood it.

This shift of religion from the outer to the inner sphere, which made the introduction of tolerance easier, proceeded relatively successfully in the Western world. This is true to the extent that Western culture, above and beyond all denominational differences, can be understood as the expression of secularised Christianity. Historically, the religious denominations of the West adopted the same "Protestant" version of religion insofar as they withdrew to varying extents from the public sphere and thus from politics. This holds true for the Christian denominations as well as for the reformed and conservative variants of the Jewish faith, which was transformed by and large in the same way. But it also holds true for a Catholicism that adopted a system of denominations that corresponds to Protestantism. Such a "protestantisation" of religion proved most successful in the United States, where religion as a personal creed compensates extensively for its banishment from the public sphere, its separation from politics, by means of a very special popularity in the private domain.

Whether such transformation of religion into a personal creed can be valid for Islam has not yet been established, although the many versions of Islam do not permit an apodictic judgement. However, one could take the following into consideration: that the religion of Muslims comes up against two obstacles in the process of shifting from the political to the inner, the personal level. First of all, there is the fact that although the culture of the West is secular, it is of Christian provenance. For Islam, a civilisation that historically has juxtaposed itself to Christianity and the West, the adoption of that secularised, yet originally Christian form, may affect its theologically-based feeling of superiority. For Islam - the last revealed monotheistic religion – considers itself a cut above its predecessors, Judaism and Christianity. Moreover, Islam experienced secularisation only to a limited extent. At any rate, such a proto-secularisation was considerably hindered by the stipulation of a divine unity of religion and state – a unity that was shattered in Christendom, i.e. in the West, by a process of upheaval and rejection in early-modern times.

However, even a dogmatic interpretation of Islam should not lead us to think that the written word is everything. Where Muslims live in large numbers in a democratic, pluralistic society, reality is quite different – for example in India, whose Muslim population is even larger than that in the Islamic state of Pakistan. As citizens of the largest democracy in the world, Muslims there are very much integrated into society and play a major role in the public sphere. Of course, India's Muslims have always lived in a socially complex and pluralistic polity of many religions, of social, linguistic and ethnic groups. However, apart from those who live in disputed regions like Kashmir, in which the homogeneity of the Muslim population seems to lend itself, as it were, to a narrow ethnocentric linking of religion to territory, India's Muslims prefer democratic and pluralistic integration.

It is in the countries of the West, where Muslims arrived as emigrants, that an Islamic self-image based on a dogmatic interpretation of religious texts evolved. It would appear that where there is no pragmatic and established tradition of everyday life, there is a stronger likelihood that recent and often alienated newcomers will resort to the religious texts, falling back on a radical interpretation of the written word. Migration to the West can thus have two consequences: an alienation that responds by the radicalisation of one's faith, but also a religion that adopts the principles of a personal faith, of a religious denomination.

The more diverse a society is in terms of religions and ethnic communities, the more necessary it becomes to internalise or neutralise the visible expressions of affiliation. The extent of such a transformation determines the level of tolerance. In the United States, whose population is basically made up of "foreigners", i.e. immigrants, refugees, and their children, it is a matter of keeping the public sphere free of emblems of affiliation in order to ensure successful co-existence. It is precisely this neutralisation that enables American patriotism to rest on principles alone – the principle of freedom and the principle of civil liberties. In terms of religion or ethnicity, civil liberties are, so to speak, "colour-blind", and thus ultimately universal.

The neutralisation of people's origins as a pre-condition for the institutional tolerance of others may have been easy to accomplish in terms of turning religion into a personal creed, i.e. in terms of its "protestantisation". However, the internalisation of symbols of ethnic affiliation, the emblems of one's origins, is another matter altogether. The constitution of the United States creates the socio-political phenomena of distance and indifference that produce the above-mentioned "colour-blindness". Distance and indifference in the public sphere are regulatory mechanisms in a political system that is based exclusively on institutions and procedures. The prerequisite for participation in such a regulatory system is freedom, liberty, and equality before the law. And everything that serves the interests of the equality of the individual, of the citizen, is also in the interests of common peace under the law. In the United States, the land of the future and the commonwealth that is best able to offer a home and security to people from the most varied origins, naturalisation neutralises origins, while this neutralisation is accomplished through procedures. It is through procedures that the individual makes his previous affiliation invisible, and also through procedures that he becomes American. Up until the 1960s, it was felt that a reduction of differences could be achieved through the American concept of the "melting pot". In the past two decades, however, that concept has given way to a very different one: visibility is once again coming to the fore in the hyphenisation of Americans. In other words, by means of a hyphen, an affiliation with an ethnic touch has been constructed below the level of citizenship. It is the hyphen which gives a fundamental meaning to being an American: the citizen committed to the constitution and to procedures.

The allusion to a preceding origin contained in the designation Afro-American, Irish-American, Muslim-American etc. creates neither a political, nor a territorial nor a public sphere for the neutralised expressions of origin. At most, such an allusion can be understood as having mere cultural significance. "American-ness", on the other hand, which is what really counts in the functioning of the body politic, is expressed solely in procedures, which find themselves symbolised in the hyphen positioned between the designation of origin and that of citizenship.

With its separation of citizenship and origin – regardless of whether origin is defined in terms of religion or ethnicity – America, the United States, is showing the way to the rest of the world. While its openness towards origin was inevitable in a New World of immigrants and refugees, the old worlds are having a more difficult time. Despite all the openness imposed on them by current circumstances, they tend to stick to their religious or ethnic origins. To that extent, they are exclusive rather than inclusive. And their level of tolerance towards the Other in their midst is therefore much lower than the level in America. The claim that comparative harmony reigns in traditional societies is by and large misleading. After all, as far as origin in terms of religious and ethnic affiliations is concerned, the level of openness and acceptance in America is far greater than it is in Europe. Paradoxically, what makes matters more difficult in some European countries is the tradition of social security, a welfare system which favours citizens on the basis of entitlement or even origin. Entitlement is based on time spent in the country, a luxury denied newcomers to those countries. The result is that countries of the old world are more inclined to reject would-be immigrants than is America, which recognises a constitution but not people's origins.

Various forms of globalisation confront the world's communities with the pros and cons of an open society. Higher economic growth belongs to the advantages, while an increasing social divide between rich and poor belongs to the drawbacks. Additionally, increasing openness demands a greater degree of tolerance. Tolerance can be brought about not so much by improving people's nature as by establishing institutions that regulate diversity. Regulation, in turn, is based first and foremost on neutralising the diversities of origin – be they ethnic or religious. This could have been learned from John Locke long ago.

Dan Diner
Historian and writer.

Born in 1946 in Munich. Assistant Professor at the Hebrew University, Jerusalem. Director of the Simon Dubnow-Institute for Jewish History and Culture at the University of Leipzig.

Selected publications: *Zivilsationsbruch. Denken nach Auschwitz* (1989); *Der Krieg der Erinnerungen und die Ordnung der Welt* (1991); *Kreisläufe. Nadtionalsozialismus und Gedächtnis* (1995); *Das Jahrhundert verstehen. Eine universalhistorische Deutung* (1999); *Beyond the Conceivable. Studies on Germany, Nazism and the Holocaust* (2001).

Return to Islamic Roots

A Conversation

In your opinion, what are the prerequisites for tolerance?

It seems to me that from an individual perspective – and that is the perspective adopted by the writer – tolerance always emerges out of respect for the other. The other may be someone familiar, a friend, a foreigner, but at times it can be an adversary, an enemy. Respect for the other presupposes that a person has considerable self-awareness, and has certain guaranteed rights, namely autonomy and freedom.

Is it then individual interpersonal relationships or rather political structures which determine how much tolerance is actually feasible in a society?

Tolerance follows respect as a second step. Tolerance exists in the context of collectives, independent groups or nations. Thus, for someone who lives under an unjust, abusive authority, survival and the fight for personal identity are primary concerns. Let me give you an example: tolerance is not high on the list of priorities of a woman who is suppressed, who may not move about freely, who has no self-determination, whose only experience of the other is one of fear and the constraints of obedience ... If recognition of the other comes only through fear, the primary impulse is to fight, openly or secretly, in order to regain autonomy. So today, many of those who live under dictatorial conditions, many women who have to live with discrimination and gender apartheid, are inclined to misinterpret morality and religion. Tolerance is a relevant topic for debate in a democratic context only where individual freedom is recognized and respected.

Is it not true that followers of certain Islamic movements, structurally authoritarian as they are, plead for a return to the original ideals of religion, where tolerance is paramount?

It is obvious that over the past twenty years, religious movements in the current Islamic world – particularly in Africa, the Middle East, Iran and Pakistan – have become increasingly orthodox, but in a way which completely distorts the original Islam since they champion an intolerable degree of Puritanism ...

... as well as a tremendous amount of violence ...

There are Islamic movements dedicated to peace and others inclined to violence. The popularity of the latter has to be understood as a product which has developed out of the dissatisfaction of people living under corrupt governments. If one sees how some corrupted minorities have grown richer in these authoritarian pseudo-democratic states, one could be led to believe that a policy which claims to be based on Islamic values could lead to social justice. But what this policy actually produces is violence, a restriction of the rights of women and, in many countries, of the rights of non-Muslim minorities.

Is this also the background of the violence that the people in your homeland Algeria have to suffer?

230   Since 1992, the attacks on freedom in Algeria have claimed
more than a hundred thousand lives, most of them civilians.
Thanks to resistance on the part of intellectuals, women, and
a number of political parties, it has been possible to prevent
my country from becoming a non-democratic Islamic republic. Our constitution grants equality to all, men and women;
the Muslim religion is considered to be that of the majority of
the population. Nevertheless, we still have a long way to go
to bring about the separation of politics and religion – a separation which in my opinion is a prerequisite for much-
needed structural reform, as well as for an open Islam which
strives for political and social equality and the toleration of
minorities.

*You have mentioned peace-oriented religious movements.
How can you win support for the original messages of Islam
which propagate ways of life and forms of government aimed
at the welfare of all members of the community?*

I believe that this can be achieved only through better knowledge and understanding of our history. Knowledge about the
true Islam, with its intellectual rigor and its respect for minorities, should immediately be added to the school curriculum at all levels. Tolerance begins with the knowledge of
one's own heritage.

What then should students in your homeland be taught?

In North Africa we should be disciples or at least constant
readers of Ibn Roushd, commentator of Aristotle, whose critical spirit was familiar in Europe's oldest universities. We
should be admirers of Ibn Arabi, the poet, mystic, and
philosopher who influenced Dante. We are the children of
Ibn Kaldoun, the founder of modern sociology who was
born in Tunisia and died in Cairo. We can turn to prestigious
forefathers who have influenced the thinking of the world.

Would these lessons include at least one chapter on how to encounter the other?

Originally, meeting the other appeared in Islam as a transmission of traditional wisdom. But then along came the European crusaders, and the open Islamic approach encountered stark violence. Ransacking, plundering, burning, raping, waging war, conquering and taking possession of sanctuaries, the Crusaders brought with them the very opposite of tolerance. It was not the spiritual treasures of the Muslims they were interested in, but rather their wealth and possessions. During the Inquisition, after the fall of Granada, the fleeing Jews fortunately found refuge in the cities of the Ottoman Empire. In this context, we should talk about the intolerance of Christian monotheism, whose spirit was corrupted. Ultimately, every religion has served as a justification for the worst and for the best.

You teach female creative writing in the Department of Romance Languages at New York University. What is the most important guidance you offer your students?

First of all, I try to teach them how to read. The ability to read then creates in them a need to write, first about themselves and then about others. This is the first intellectual step in what I call the "pedagogy of tolerance". Writing helps a woman, even a suppressed woman, to discover her creativity and to draw her personality and inner integrity from it. In this sense, writing engenders courage. Constructing fictional characters provides insights into the lives of others. Writing novels and plays enables the author to move beyond her own reality, to leave her problems and the inner prison behind and to reach out to others.

In conversation with Angela Grünert.

232   **Assia Djebar**
        Writer. Winner of the Peace Prize of the Association of the
        German Book Industry (2000).

        Born in 1936 in Cherchell near Algier. The first Algerian
        woman to be admitted into the exclusive Ecole Normale
        Supérieure in Paris. Lecturer in French Studies at New York
        University. Currently rated as the top female writer in the
        Maghreb.

        Selected publications: *Femmes d'Alger dans leur appartement*
        (1980); *L'Amour, la fantasia* (1985); *Vaste est la prison* (1995);
        Le blanc d'Algérie (1996); *Oran, langue morte* (1997).

MAHMOUD ZAKZOUK

ISLAM: SOURCE OF TOLERANCE

As a global religion, Islam appeals for universal tolerance. With the gap between cultures shrinking, Islam's message is addressed to all of mankind, which now more than ever needs to learn how to deal with tolerance. The goal of Islam is to help its followers learn to become global citizens who think in an open-minded and tolerant way and act in a responsible manner.

Islam teaches us that we are responsible for our planet Earth. We have to manage and protect God's creation lovingly and respectfully. It is with this purpose that God has sent us to Earth as His deputies (The Koran, Suras 2,31; 33, 72). Instead of causing mischief and spilling blood on Earth, man should remember his true task, which he – if he really tries – can accomplish by applying the power of reason granted to him (Sura 2,30/31). This is why the Koran constantly appeals to man's reason and urges him to assert his freedom, since a man's creativity is more important to God than his blind obedience. Rather than waste his limited freedom, man should attain creative freedom through self-education (i.e., by thinking and acting reasonably).

Self-education teaches him tolerance and allows him to correctly assess his own abilities.

An awareness of our own shortcomings and our own responsibilities (which are essential for human dignity) makes it possible for us to treat people whose lives cross ours both generously and tolerantly. Tolerance implies a natural recognition of the dignity and freedom of every individual as long as he does not break any laws. The awareness that we are imperfect means we cannot be certain that we are always right and always know the truth. This in turn requires that, as a matter of principle, we have to be tolerant of every individual – whatever race, nation, culture, religion or creed he belongs to. It is important to bear in mind that (most) people assume a group identity under peer pressure, they do not seek it out by themselves.

This, in sum, is the definition of universal tolerance which Islam sets down as one of the conditions for attaining the peace necessary for community life. It is also the proper way for a man to behave, the way blessed by our Creator, the way that accepts and respects the diversity of cultures and the uniqueness of an individual.

Thus, tolerance is based on the premise that a man makes a conscious effort to behave in a just and fair way. For if a man shows tolerance only for the sake of personal benefit and not for the sake of fairness, such tolerance is a shame. The Koran provides us with an example of what we could call "active tolerance", which amounts to more than mere sufferance: "Allah forbideth you not those who warred not against you on account of religion and drove you not out from your homes, that ye should show them kindness and deal justly with them. Lo! Allah loveth the just dealers." (Sura 60, 8)

We should look closer at the way the Koran phrases its wisdom here. As elsewhere, it resorts to subtle hints rather than to orders. As a matter of principle, the Koran offers a gradual solution for every kind of a problem and a step-by-step explanation for every message it contains, both in keeping with the level of its reader's education. For Islam discourages the attempt to learn the Koran mechanically or the blindly obedient acting-out of its commandments. Rather, it promotes self-education and self-realisation, encouraging people to act out of the confidence they have thereby acquired and which is therefore just and fair. The Koran text cited above is the first reference to the fact that God has not prohibited tolerance. The second reference indicates that tolerance of others can only be just. Compulsory tolerance in religious and moral matters can achieve nothing, since enforcement usually brings about the opposite of what is desired. The Koran also teaches that every man is free to decide for himself whether tolerant behaviour vis-à-vis others is justified. Educating oneself and developing an ability to act responsibly is possible only when a person learns to think freely and act reasonably.

The diversity of the groups formed by others should not stop us from learning more about them and showing tolerance towards them. How else can we cope with our duty to be Allah's representatives in this world? Moreover, it is precisely this human diversity that makes it possible for us to reach the goal Allah has set us. For the efforts needed to understand others – an understanding we can aspire to only if we are deeply rooted in our own culture – require the ability to tolerate others. Only thus do we have the chance to learn about others and to act responsibly and reasonably – in other words, to develop a truly human touch. This is what the Koran says about it: "O mankind! Lo! We have created you male and female, and have made you nations and tribes that ye may know one another. Lo! The noblest of you, in the sight of Allah, is the best in conduct. Lo! Allah is Knower, Aware." (Sura 49, 13)

Since people have to communicate with each other, in spite of – or even because of – all their disparities, Islam was the first of all religions to call for an interfaith dialogue, as it proclaimed: "Call unto the way of the Lord with wisdom and fair exhortation, and reason with them the better way. Lo! Thy Lord is best aware of him who strayeth from His way, and He is Best Aware of those who go aright." (Sura 16, 125)

236   This means we should let Allah judge our contemporaries. For our part, we should make an effort to be fair to and tolerant of them. Religion holds us responsible for our actions. That is why the Koran says: "I believe in whatever Scripture Allah hath sent down, and I am commanded to be just among you. Allah is our Lord and your Lord. Unto us our works and unto you your works; no argument between us and you. Allah will bring us together, and unto Him is the journeying." (Sura 42, 15)

This brings us to the issue of tolerance in a more narrow sense, i.e., the issue of religious tolerance. One of the religious precepts in Islam considers all revelationary faiths to be equally valid roads leading to God. This means that Muslims have to respect equally all the prophets who have appeared since the dawn of mankind – prophets such as, for instance, Moses and Jesus.

Consequently, we can read in our history books that the Prophet Mohammed practiced religious tolerance and the freedom of worship – i.e., upheld religious and cultural pluralism. The Caliphs, especially Caliph Omar, followed his example. History books are full of stories about the generous religious tolerance practiced by Sultan Saladdin. In its entire history, Islam has never been imposed by force (and a number of Western scholars have confirmed this). Rather, Islam has been known to defend – especially during its peak period – the freedom of worship and other human rights. To this day, Jews and Christians are equal to Muslims in the countries ruled by Islamic governments and they have in principle the same rights and obligations as Muslims.

I have attempted to explain that active tolerance, be it in universal or religious matters, is one of the goals of a (properly understood) Islamic education. I have also tried to make clear where the limits of such tolerance lie. Tolerance stops wherever opposing goals are pursued, wherever people are no longer treated in a just and fair manner, in short, wherever human rights – be they one's own or those of others – are abused.

For we can defend human rights only by becoming personally involved, since state laws (which, of course, are necessary) are unable to ensure their full protection. This is why the Prophet Mohammed says: "He who sees an evil doing should correct it with his own hand. If he cannot do so, then he should use his tongue. If he cannot do so either, he should use his heart. This, however, is the weakest form of faith." Thus, there is no tolerance of injustice and cruelty under Islam.

To conclude, let me tell you a typical old Islamic story which provides a good example of active Islamic tolerance. The story tells of an episode from the life of the second Caliph Omar. One day he saw an old man begging on the street corner and was told that he was a Jew. The Caliph was saddened by the old man's misfortune and said that such things should not be happening in his state. Therefore he ordered that the old Jew be given a state pension, so that he would be assured a decent means of subsistence in his old age.

From the same Caliph we have inherited a famous saying: "How come people are enslaved again and again, if they were born free?"

This, from the Islamic point of view, is the key task of mankind: to lead the struggle for the freedom of man, to fight in solidarity with others, a solidarity which embraces universal and religious tolerance.

Mahmoud Zakzouk
Minister of Religious Affairs of Egypt.

Born in 1933 in Dakahleya. Received Ph. D. in Philosophy in Munich in 1968. Former Vice President of Al-Azhar University; Dean of the Faculty of Islamic Theology (Ussoul El-Din); Head of the Islamic Thought Committee of the Supreme Council for Islamic Affairs; Minister of Religious Endowments. Representative of the Grand Imam of Al-Azhar University at international conferences and symposia.

A Plea for A Reform Islam

A Euro-Islamic Vision

Setting: a synagogue in Westminster, London. Jews and Muslims have come here to set up the Jewish-Muslim Dialogue, a joint initiative for a better intercultural understanding. As the discussion starts, a rabbi gets up to thank Muslims for having saved Jewish lives from Christian murderers – long, long ago in Moorish Spain – by treating them as "Dhimmi" (wards-of-the-state). Then he adds proudly: "But times have changed." These days the Jews don't want to be viewed as wards-of-the-state. "The Jews would like to be recognised as a sovereign people. Can Muslims in this day and age offer the kind of tolerance that will accord the Jews that recognition?"

I'm starting my article with the story about the Jewish-Muslim Dialogue, which I helped organise[1], to demonstrate the problems confronting a traditional Muslim concept of tolerance.[2] It would be wrong to describe Islam as a generally "tolerant religion" without adding that Islam is prepared to put up with – and give legal protection to – only followers of other monotheistic faiths, such as the Christians and the Jews.

While tolerated by Islam, these people enjoy fewer rights than the full members of "Umma" (the Islamic community); Buddhists, Hindus and believers in other religions – as well as atheists and agnostics – are barely tolerated, and Muslims

who would like to leave the Islamic community are not tolerated at all.

Compared with the Islamic notion of toleration, the contemporary concept of enlightened tolerance[3] offers other
faiths and ideologies, whether they are religious or secular,
more freedom and respect. What that very liberal Reform
rabbi said above only goes to show that Muslims find themselves under pressure to review, revise and adjust their orthodox concept of tolerance. To begin with, Muslims have to
give up their claims to universal validity and to the pre-emi-
nence of Islam and accept that Islam is part of a multicultural
world.[4] Only thus can Muslims develop a new, modern understanding of tolerance. This development has been speci-
fied in the subtitle of this article: from orthodox Islam to
Euro-Islamic tolerance.

In order to make clear what follows, let me explain two key
points on which I base my arguments for a Euro-Islamic approach:

Point One: no matter what religious persuasion or ethnic
identity people have, they share a common attitude toward
human dignity; yet, they are born and grow up in different
local cultures which have their own respective values and
views on life. Such local cultures aggregate into civilisations if
they share the same ideology. Correspondingly, people are integrated into different value systems. Within Islam, from Morocco to Indonesia[5], we encounter a great variety of cultures;
nevertheless, these numerous local cultures form a coherent
Islamic civilisation. Similarly, there is a great cultural diversity in the West which makes up Western civilisation.[6] Each
civilisation, made up of people who all share the same human
characteristics, has its own ideology. Thus, tolerance has a
different ideological meaning for Westerners and for Muslims. Here I am just stating a fact, rather than expressing an
opinion.[7] In other words, people from different civilisations
do not have the same values. Does this necessarily imply that
values are arbitrary in a culturally-relativistic sense?

240   *Point Two:* migration is part and parcel of globalization –
itself a symbol of *our times.*[8] However, while people from different cultures move together and form populations of cities,
such as Frankfurt or New York, they do not share a common
culture. Tolerance is an element of the political culture in a
civil society. Can multicultural tolerance substitute a missing
community in such a situation?

In explaining my basic premise, I am trying to show my
disagreement with Huntington's *Clash of Civilizations.*
While admitting that he is right about the conflict of cultures,
I have frequently argued that "a supra-cultural morality" is
feasible, and that it can build bridges between civilisations.[9]
In my scenario, tolerance plays a supra-cultural role as an
element of a coherent value system. Pluralism of religions and
cultures are part and parcel of such a morality.

Without Islam, it will not be possible to achieve global
peace in the 21st century. However, even with Islam, the goal
of peace will elude our grasp if we try to attain it on the basis
of a multicultural concept of arbitrary value systems, since
this concept, in the name of respect for other cultures, allows
for a type of tolerance that could lead to intolerance. As far as
Islam in Europe and specifically in Germany[10] goes, I cannot
stress often enough that tolerance, as interpreted by orthodox
Islam, has become outdated and useless, and that we cannot
permit it in a multicultural context. Toleration may have been
an advantage in the Middle Ages, but at present toleration is a
form of discrimination. Even such a reform-minded Muslim
as Abdullahi an-Na'im supports this position in his discourse
on the need for an Islamic Reformation with respect to the
position of minorities under Islam.[11]

Islamism is an excess of un-reformed orthodox Islam. As
a reform Muslim and as an enlightened proponent of many
cultures, I use my writings to warn against allowing the totalitarian ideology of Islamism[12] to grow roots in an environment of multicultural tolerance. I suggest drawing a line between Islamism as political totalitarianism and Islam as a tra-

ditionally tolerant religion, to which I also belong. Many Europeans keep talking about the need to tolerate Islamists. I am much less sanguine, because I see in my mind's eye the bloody massacres which have been taking place regularly since 1992 in Algeria, where fundamentalists have been murdering thousands of women and children, cutting their throats almost as though it were a ritual. Such murders have become so frequent and familiar to newspaper readers that the public has ceased to react with outrage. People watch the reports on television and take note of them without sympathy, almost as if they were a commercial. The U.S. media came out with their reports – dramatically headlined "Algerian Killing" – but they too fell on deadened eyes and ears. Only the attacks by Islamists in New York and Washington on September 11 awakened the world to the dangers of Islamism.

Tolerance is one of those universally valid norms and values which have made Europe into what it is today. As a liberal Muslim living in Europe, I have reason to ask whether such arch-European civilising attitudes still constitute the basis of a European defining culture? Furthermore, do Europeans distinguish between tolerance and indifference? There I have my doubts. During the events I mentioned above, Germany gave refuge to murderous fundamentalists who had been convicted as criminals in their countries. The fundamentalists were accepted as victims of political persecution. At the same time, Germany turned away the victims of fundamentalists because they were unable to prove that they too had been persecuted. Such developments only confirm my doubts, because they demonstrate to what degree German authorities lack political orientation. Before September 11, Germany was a haven for Islamic fundamentalists.[13]

The issue of tolerance as it applies to Islam, which I consider a civilisation, has to be redefined. Most refugees who are trying to get into Europe come from this Islamic civilisation. I am trying to mediate in such a critical situation by creating an environment of dialogue rather than of confrontation, and with the aim of finding a consensus on values – without our usual naivety. Yet dialogue and mediation in conflict situations such as we are experiencing cannot be conducted as harmoniously as a meeting of the local choral chapter. Dialogue involves confrontational debate, and its success requires that certain conditions and prerequisites be met. In this new situation, Europe must find a balance between the extremes of traditional high-handedness (Eurocentrism) and the abandonment of its interests out of respect (tolerance) for others; neither position is conducive to a dialogue-friendly environment. In my opinion, these are the key conditions for a viable tolerance to function at this time in history – which I call *universal time*. Orthodox Islam does not fit the parameters of such *universal time*, therefore we need Euro-Islam, a reformed version of the religion which will open it up to modern tolerance.

Viewing the un-European, i.e. Islamic-European, scene from this perspective, I have come to the conclusion that a supra-cultural morality is sorely needed. Islam is having a great impact on Europe. It is an important neighbour in the southern and eastern Mediterranean region; it is already present in Europe through migration. Following September 11, tolerance of the type "anything goes" is no longer acceptable. For this reason, I advocate a defining culture of tolerance.

For us to co-exist in peace, we need to overcome our differences in a rational way and to come to a consensus over norms and values; both are necessary in order for us to be able to practice tolerance. Only if we recognise differences and are able to talk about them can we reach a consensus. This, in turn, will make it possible for people to have different views of themselves and of the world – I call the latter civilising philosophies of life. The aspects of modern culture which help maintain internal and social peace in Europe provide the basis for a commonality of values, which amounts to what I call "a defining culture."

My idea of a consensus-based, yet markedly European defining culture applies exclusively to Europe. As a bridge-builder, however, I recommend that Europe, in dealing with its non-European neighbours, reaffirm its own identity while looking for new ways to recognise others. In dealing with other cultures, Europe must learn to accept supra-cultural patterns, or what I would call international supra-cultural morality.

Let me summarise: *within Europe, we need to share with immigrants a defining culture that is based on a value consensus; outside Europe, we need an international morality. In the first case, the value consensus must be European; in the second, it must be supra-cultural.* Only within such a framework can tolerance function in our *universal time.* Unlike orthodox Islamic ideology, Euro-Islam can be brought into harmony with this interpretation of a European defining culture. However, such a defining culture of tolerance, which should evolve out of a dialogue between Europeans and non-European immigrants, must set limits on attempts by the latter to affirm their cultural values in Europe. In the context of religious tolerance – and I write this as a Muslim – there can be no place in Europe for "Shari'a" (Islamic religious law). Yet Islamists, in the name of communitarian rights and the self-given right to their own, self-created cultural identity, would like to install "Shari'a" among Muslims who have immigrated to Europe. My counter-argument is: "Shari'a" is at odds with the secular identity of Europe and is diametrically opposed to secular European constitutions formulated by the people. An alternative to the neo-absolutism of Islamists is an intercultural dialogue that searches for communalities and thus requires a cultural awareness and the willingness to compromise as indications of the mutual ability to conduct such a dialogue. The separation of religion from politics and the validity of individual human rights are not up for negotiation even in the name of tolerance, because abandoning these values would amount to giving up the entire European civilisation, whose secularity forms the basis for the practice of religious pluralism.

It is important for me to remind the reader again that this call for a defining culture is coming from a Semitic Arab who belongs to an Islamic civilisation; who is an immigrant and would like to be a European, which means that he, as an alien, is fighting for recognition and acceptance.[14] Being what I am, I believe that modern European culture can provide the defining culture described above. In short: I hold out for the superiority of common sense over religious faith (i.e. absolute religious precepts); *individual* human rights (i.e. not collective human rights); secular democracy based on the separation of religion from politics; a *universally accepted* pluralism; and a mutually accepted secular tolerance. The acceptance of these values is the foundation of a civil society.[15] I believe that a reformed Islam can lead to a Euro-Islam that would open the Islamic diaspora to the pluralistic spirit of European tolerance and enlightenment.

NOTES

1 On this Jewish-Muslim dialogue, cf. B. Tibi, *Krieg der Zivilisationen. Politik und Religion zwischen Vernunft und Fundamentalismus* (first edition 1995), extended version, Munich 1998. With a new introduction after September 11: Munich 2001, here p. 291.

2 More about this in Adel Khoury, *Toleranz im Islam*, Mainz 1980.

3 Werner Becker, "Toleranz: Grundwert der Demokratie?", in: *Ethik und Sozialwissenschaften*, Vol. 8 (1997), 4, pp. 413–423.

4 On pluralism cf. John Keks, *The Morality of Pluralism*, Princeton 1993. On cultural pluralism cf. Monique Deveaux, *Cultural Pluralism and Dilemma of Justice*, Ithaca 2000. Different in B. Tibi, *Europa ohne Identität? Die Krise der multikulturellen Gesellschaft*, München 1998, (paperback edition, Berlin 2000 und 2001), chapter 4.

5 Clifford Geertz, *Religiöse Entwicklungen im Islam beobachtet in Marokko und Indonesien*, Frankfurt 1988 (new 1991), with a new essay by B. Tibi.

6 Leslie Lipson also views Islam as a coherent civilisation in his seminal book: *The Ethical Crisis of Civilization*, London 1993; on Islam pp. 78, on the West pp. 41.

7 This is also the key concept of my book *Krieg der Zivilisationen* (cf. fn. 1). Islamic ideology is examined in each of the following chapters: State, Law, Religion, War/Peace und Knowledge.

8 This is important: Myron Weiner, *The Global Migration Crisis*, New York 1995.

9 B. Tibi, "International Morality and Cross-Cultural Bridging", in: Roman Herzog, *Preventing the Clash of Civilizations*, New York 1999, pp. 107–126.

10 B. Tibi, Der Islam und Deutschland. Muslime in Deutschland, München 2000, new edition 2001.

11 Abdullahi an-Na'im, *Toward an Islamic Reformation*, Syracuse 1990, especially pp. 161.

12 Cf. B. Tibi, *Fundamentalismus im Islam. Eine Gefahr für den Weltfrieden?*, Darmstadt 2000 (new edition 2001).

13 Cf. Stefan Theil, "Tolerating the Untolerable", in: Newsweek of 5 November 2001, pp. 46–47.

14 Jürgen Habermas, *Die Einbeziehung des Anderen*, Frankfurt 1996.

15 Cf. the discussion on this issue in the collection of articles by John Hall (ed.), *Civil Society. Theory, History, Comparison*, Cambridge 1996.

Bassam Tibi
Sociologist and historian. Professor of International Relations at Göttingen University.

Born in 1944 in Damaskus. Studied philosophy, sociology and history in Germany. Founder of "Islamology", an area of studies focusing on the sociology of Islam. Professorships at Harvard 1988–1993, Berkeley 1994, and Ankara 1995.

Selected publications: *Arab Nationalism: Between Islam and the Nation State* (1997); *The Challenge of Fundamentalism: Political Islam and the New World Disorder* (1998); *Islam between Culture and Politics* (2001); *Krieg der Zivilisationen. Politik und Religion zwischen Vernunft und Fundamentalismus* (1995, 1998); *Europa ohne Identität? Die Krise der mulitkulturellen Gesellschaft* (1998); *Kreuzzug und Djihad. Der Islam und die christliche Welt* (1999); *Fundamentalismus im Islam. Eine Gefahr für den Weltfrieden?* (2000); *Der Islam und Deutschland. Muslime in Deutschland* (2000).

SIBYLLE LEWITSCHAROFF

ON INDULGENCE

"Let us not forget that a man can, rather easily, imagine himself in another person's position or even within that person's mind. If he does so, then it should not be too difficult for him to accept the other person's understanding and perception of the divine, the perception formed by that person's very specific attitude to the rest of the world. Yet, such perceptions should not be formed by a life of impulsive arrogance or servility which tend to make the spirit so miserable and violent that it would always reveal itself either as a tyrant or as a slave ...

Thus, we can accept the other person's pure vision of the divine, however limited it may be, just as we can accept the other's simple but pure way of life. Indeed, as long as people do not feel offended or angry, depressed or mad over a just or unjust conflict, they have a basic need to join their differing perceptions of God, so that they can be free to indulge themselves, each one in his own way, in enjoying their naturally and inevitably limited vision of the divine spirit ..."

Hölderlin, *Philosophical Letters, A Fragment*

Tolerance creates a special state of mind which helps a person explore another's inner being. Tolerance frees the mind to float into another's body and return, inspired. But this can happen only to those who are at peace with their fellows. And since such a happy, unforced and violence-free state seldom occurs, tolerance in its inspired form is rare indeed.

In the 19th century people still believed that this kind of inspired tolerance would blossom by itself. Education, enhanced knowledge, travel, and international contacts would help spread civilised customs across the globe. No one could imagine that a century later, fanatics would violently wreck Europe and other parts of the world. After the Second World War, the mood of tolerance that Western nations worked hard to re-establish was not "inspired" at all.

Hölderlin wrote about gentler, timeless notions. A celestial sheen envelops them in his works. Inspired tolerance reposes on a sunny, wooded hillside, with slowly-meandering brooks and gentle slopes curving into lightly intoxicating air. Those who find their way to this inspired tolerance wander around, talk to and honour each other, each man a part of something greater, to be appreciated by others. These people and their spiritual transformations are just a small part of the divine creation. Books are scattered on the hillside, inviting passers-by to peek inside. Even the tales of the dead can thus enrich human exchanges.

The other side of the hill is strewn with ugly stones. This is the home of modern tolerance, devoid of divine inspiration and therefore indifferent to everything. Goethe wrote that Frau von Laroche appeared to be involved in everything around her, yet remained entirely unaffected. Modern city dwellers are much the same when they attempt to walk amidst the cacophony of people speaking many languages, making noises and arguing, challenging and imploring each other, giving and asking for advice. Open your ears to this babble and your eyes to the scenes incessantly attacking your senses and you might go mad.

The present world is divided into two parts: one is a wasteland of limitless possibilities, where the kin of Frau von Laroche feel fully at home; the other is home to the disciples of the bloody faith, bending deep over a single text. The face of God, watching the former, is pale and hard to recognise; the face of Mars, glaring down on the latter, is a furious red mask.

The wasteland crowd, constipated from over-consumption, no longer knows rest or the tranquillity necessary to ensure the success of a creative act, or the repose that borders on melancholy, yet is vital for replenishing energy and renewing creativity. Melancholia-sufferers of various persuasions no longer seem able to meet and talk about the sadness reigning at the secret source of creation. Meanwhile, the disciples of the bloody faith communicate only with their own; they rest not but clamour for death.

Tolerance implies indulgence. It embraces benevolence, leniency, gentleness, caution, forbearance, and, in extreme cases, the patience of a saint. The most pious men are blessed by it. Asians, Stoics and wise men, all who possess an inner sense of peace are able to practice tolerance. A tolerant person is indulgent, charitable, benevolent, circumspect, sensible, peace-loving, relaxed, patient, moderate, careful, forbearing, open-hearted, generous, sober under the best of circumstances and responsible, but mostly weak and indifferent.

A short-tempered, cantankerous person is rarely perceived as tolerant. Scorching anger, smouldering fury, hate that keeps (like a lava tongue) bursting out in flames; a way of thinking so rigid that every new sentence is poured in concrete – all these have little to do with tolerance.

Perhaps tolerance can be practiced only in a state of dull sleepiness that softens our perception of continuity and permeates our personal and temporal continuums as if they were translucent onion rings. Musil's pondering the limits of possibilities leads to tolerance. Walker Percy's works are saturated with it. And Proust couches it in intricate terms of compassion.

Does this mean there is literature, modern literature at that, that could inspire tolerance? This is a tricky question. Despite the existence of exalted fiction, connoisseur-only concerts and a monstrously revered Hölderlin in the Hitler years, the German bourgeoisie failed to perceive the brutality of the Nazis. The post-war generation, in a fit of denial, could not think of anything better to do than to destroy the tradition of education while viewing those who sought to escape into it as ludicrous philistines.

Nevertheless, I am convinced that some books have a kind of power that helps instil tolerance. I always think of Kafka in such a context. No other writer is less able to serve inhuman causes. Kafka yields neither to an exalted overview by an indifferent observer nor to a teary embrace by an emotional reader. He has a very dry and precise approach to things. For years, critics have focused on his penchant for the dark aspects of life. These days there is a tendency to emphasize his humorous side, his almost cinematographic world of characters, his Chaplin-like vision of the world delivered through literature. These are all exaggerations. His ability to integrate humour with sadness and wisdom remains unrivalled. His wisdom is delivered with head-spinning sharpness and is aimed at the invisible walls of a godless world.

His prose assiduously pursues the biblical theme of Job and his quest for an answer to the "Why" question. "Job-the-Edomite is not looking for justice. He would be doing so if he were a Jew. No, Job-the-Edomite is trying to make sense of things. He demands that God *give him wisdom*. ... Fully rejecting Augustine view 'If you understand it, it is not God,' Job is screaming for God to reveal Himself as someone less incredibly absurd than He appears to be." (George Steiner, *Grammars of Creation*, London 2001). To go one step further, we could say that Kafka, like a detective, pursues the traces that God left behind as He was withdrawing from the world He had created, God's traces that make us feel angry rather than happy, the traces that leave Kafka's characters muttering darkly or shaking their fists, powerless. One thing is clear: there is no salvation for anyone. Every Kafka story which deals with salvation ends with a rejection. Amongst writers Kafka is the huge bat which keeps emitting piercing squeaks into God's darkness and keeps straining its big ears, trying to catch the answer. Kafka's style makes the storyteller stand out like a bas-relief, the front surface lit up, the rest of the body remaining in the shadows. It is somewhat similar to the way the prophets of the Old Testament spoke, but is more effective. The Bible can no longer console anyone, in the worst case it even foments hatred. Kafka's style of story-telling does console his readers, because today, artistic expression consoles more than the word of God. Any story by Kafka can easily compete with a biblical story. Moses and the Ten Commandments? Kafka's story *The Judgment* tells us more. Jacob and his sons? I prefer *Eleven Sons*. The parable of the generous Samaritan? *The Bucket Rider* is better.

Kafka's language has the priceless advantage of being able to project consummate non-violence. Naturally, his stories talk about people getting beaten, bitten, tortured and killed. But his texts do not appeal to the reader's aggressive instincts. Martin Luther's writings, on the other hand, are quite the opposite. His earthiness, his frenzy, his dogmatism and his zest for action are palpable in his writings to this day. Violent energy infuses his language, irritates the reader and brings out his own dogmatism. If there were a way to measure aggressive brain emanations during reading, then we would give test participants an excerpt from Luther's translation of the Old Testament and then the same text in the strange, flowery translation by Buber and Rosenzweig. We would see sharp spikes on the screens during the first half of the experiment and calm, wavelike fluctuations during the second.

During the reading of *A Country Doctor,* the reader would be excited only by the unexpected twists in Kafka's phrasing, twists that surprise even someone who has read them before. Kafka's fussy conscientiousness, which comes through in all of his texts, is free from the Protestant need for domination. He does not force his way of exploring conscience on anyone, no one is required to imitate it. Instead, conscience comes through as a curse. He closely examines actions and motives, searching for even the smallest shred of guilt. Yet such guilt, more guessed at than proved, is never enough to justify the grinding wheels of fortune that magically reappear in front of Kafka's characters wherever they turn.

He works wonders through entirely fictitious characters. Their flesh is hidden from us. Their overall image remains blurred. Yet certain details stand out with the sharp precision of reality. There is not a single character in Kafka's books who reminds us of men of flesh and blood. Because of their abstract, ephemeral nature, such characters can be more convincing to a reader than people portrayed realistically with skin and hair and flowing juices. And then there are the many creatures that move somewhere between man-beast and lifeless life forms: a ball that leads a life of its own; Odradek, a dirty spool of thread; untameable horses which rage around like the steeds of Titans and suddenly slither about as if their bones were made of rubber. They are the only creatures that come alive under Kafka's careful pen.

But even Kafka cannot help those who see the world through an icy prism of one single theory and who prefer staying in a prison of their own egos. Such people would not even be able to read Kafka, would not possess the gentle, inner peace that is necessary for his texts to make any impact.

A hothead could be helped only if Prof. Dr. Horn had treated him. Who is Dr. Horn? A medical expert, a hulk of a man, he receives his little patients in a snow-white gown, charms them thoroughly and then starts treating their rage symptoms. A clamp is applied to a patient's nose as he is led around to thundering chords of the *Coronation March* from the opera *The Prophet* by Giacomo Meyerbeer. The patient must then pour out his rage until it becomes a true-blue, pulsating wrath. All the while, the professor marches behind the patient, beating him on the head rhythmically with leather-clad hammers and drumsticks. The aim of this therapy is to bring rage to the boiling point. When this happens, porcelain figurines are smashed onto the floor. Towards the end of the treatment, the patient becomes exhausted and completely harmless. Dr. Horn is a creation of Heimito von Doderer and appears in his novel *The Merovingians or the Total Family*. Doderer himself suffered from fits of uncontrolled rage, and was therefore an expert on anger. This expertise manifests itself in his delectable short and shortest stories with such meaningful titles as *The Affliction of Leather Pouches* or *The Eight Fits of Rage*.

Actually, I have a temper that is very similar to Doderer's; I was about to say we are comrades-in-temper. So I would not mind flying into rage together with him. Except that it would not work. A hothead should blow up alone. Others are just there to tame him.

In short, I am grateful to Doderer for the insights he has provided into the origins of blind rage and for suggesting ways to cope with that rage. Yet it is to Kafka that I fully owe the fact that, despite my rather fractious nature, I do not always get mad but am relatively civilised and even tolerant at times. Kafka's prose influences me the way the Bible should affect a Christian: it indulges me, it softens my temper and makes me feel wise and reserved, broad-minded, level-headed and patient, even though, clearly, this does not last for ever.

Sibylle Lewitscharoff
Writer. Winner of the Ingeborg Bachmann Prize (1998) for her book *Pong*.

Born in 1954 in Stuttgart. Studied religion in Berlin.

Selected publications: *36 Gerechte* (1994); *Im Schrank* (1996, radio play); *Der höfliche Harald* (1999) – a children's book with her own illustrations, received an award from the Foundation for Publishing Arts.

VIVIANE SENNA

GLOBAL PANACEAS: ETHICS AND RELIGION

The first human inroads into the New Millennium leave no doubt that we have embarked on an era which will be characterised by deep and irreversible interdependence between nations. An interdependence generated by economic integration, where the policies developed by rich nations have an immediate and often dramatic effect on the poorest continents; an interdependence which is vital in the effort to protect an environment which can no longer be considered local; and above all, an interdependence of thoughts and emotions.

Advances in information and communication technologies, often referred to as a revolution, give new potential to the human voice because it can reach so far and so fast, thereby making possible world-wide a form of interaction hitherto possible only in small towns or communities. But, paradoxically, by drowning out local traditions, values and cultures, this communication revolution can also endanger human intercourse and perhaps even man's very ability to survive.

On the one hand, the exercise of speech, of dialogue – considered by Aristotle to be the most remarkable ability of human kind – has never been as widely possible as it is today. A form of distance has ceased to exist, so that people in the most remote areas of the world can communicate easily.

On the other hand, despite the fact that distance no longer impedes communication and people can live far away from where they were born and educated and still preserve their identity by remaining in contact with the values and traditions of their native countries – despite this, a highly complex cultural assimilation process is taking place.

Moreover, the integration we are observing is being driven by processes which use the markets as their means, and scientific rationalism and individualism as their philosophical support. Markets, scientific rationalism and individualism certainly express a certain order of values. But these are not universal values. They are only partial expressions of the western cultural tradition, and not even the best expressions this culture has to offer.

How should we try to cope with the chaotic condition imposed by modern life? The most appropriate way is through ethics and religion. Only these can provide mankind with a counterbalance to impersonal modernity and add richness to our lives. This is true not just for distant people with distant cultures who, most threatened by modernity, seek refuge in their heritage and tradition; it is equally true for our own cultures and those of our close neighbours. We – modern mankind – are all fighting against vanity and lack of sense.

It should therefore not surprise us that the more distant cultures may not be able to identify with our global modernisation model based on western civilisation, and that they perceive risks – real or imaginary – which differ from the risks we ourselves perceive.

Different cultures have reacted in different ways. In some cases, the response has been a profound cultural and religious renewal. In others, it has been a renewal, but tragically, one characterised by sectarianism, fanaticism and violence. These responses are likely to be irreversible, even if it were possible to change the economic and technological catalysts that unleashed them. And the responses cause us to view the world and ourselves differently. Our identities change, as does the way in which we relate to 'the other'.

It is here that we need tolerance. In a pluralistic world more conscious than ever of the diversity of cultures, of traditions and of religions, a world forced to co-exist more closely than ever before, tolerance becomes the most essential of democratic virtues.

Curiously, it was the more primitive and polytheist societies of antiquity which proved to be the most tolerant, the most "democratic" in dealing with religious questions. Motivated perhaps by the principle of reciprocity, they obviously felt that dogmatism in matters of religion should be subordinated to tolerance for the sake of peaceful coexistence.

The great Brazilian theologian and thinker, Leonardo Boff, once noted that when religions turn into power institutions, whether the power be religious, social, cultural or military, they lose the spiritual source that keeps them alive and may even become, together with their dogmas, the tomb of the living God. Tolerance, that vital virtue, is a 'golden rule' of all the major religions of the world: do unto others as you would have them do unto you. This is an unconditional principle in Christianity, in Judaism, in Islam, in Buddhism, in Confucianism, in Hinduism. As a civic virtue, tolerance is also firmly established in liberal thought, which demands freedom of consciousness and autonomy of reason and allows no outside intervention.

However, as the Dalai Lama has taught us, religion can bring salvation only if it teaches man to feel a sense of responsibility towards his fellows creatures; only if principle is translated into compassion towards others who suffer, into tenderness.

While on the one hand man shows great intolerance towards the natural diversities given to us by the Creator, man shows infinite tolerance towards the unnatural diversities which he himself has created: misery and the lack of opportunities that exist in the modern world.

We can illustrate our tolerance towards these unnatural diversities by citing data published by UNRISD: in the last 30 years, the gap between income rates of the 20 percent richer population of the world and the 20 percent poorer has jumped from 30 percent to 61 percent. And the contrast is steadily increasing. But the true face of misery cannot be shown with statistics. To deprive a man of his culture is even worse than to deprive him of bread, since we refuse him the possibility of identifying an ideal. This is the reason why in a world of misery, friendship and love cannot be spread. Father Joseph Wresinski teaches that because we have been unable to be his brothers, the man of misery has become a hermit.

We must not accept the gulf between the values of tolerance, respect, justice and solidarity and the reality of life. We must make sure that the principles are implemented. They should not simply be virtues, they should be basic human rights: the right to tolerance, to respect, to dignity and to justice.

Darcy Ribeiro, the great anthropologist and politician, once stated that in terms of population and territory, Brazil is one of the greatest Latin nations. However, we are far from being a great nation in terms of our economy, social rights, science, technology, education and culture. As a nation, we are a prime example of potential that has not yet been developed.

Why? Because in the five centuries of our history, during which several races have come together (Indians, Whites and Africans) and have made us what we are today, we have been unable to guarantee to the majority of our population full access to welfare and dignity. We are therefore a country of contradictions.

If, on the one hand, we are looked to as an imperfect (albeit significant) example of the peaceful co-existence of ethnic and cultural diversities, on the other we are still a country dramatically divided into citizens and sub-citizens. Throughout our history, the dominant groups in our society have never shown any serious inclination to tackle and find solutions to the problems of social inequality. This is our greatest sin.

Despite the fact that our GDP is among the ten highest in the world, we have never been able to generate a model that could assure economic stability, social emancipation and cultural freedom to the excluded classes of our urban suburbs and sluggish rural areas.

What can we do? As Darcy Ribeiro has pointed out, two very serious questions should be asked of each Brazilian: "Why hasn't Brazil succeeded yet? What can each of us do in our own field of endeavour to ensure that Brazil succeeds?"

From its inception, the Ayrton Senna Institute has been trying to contribute an answer to these two questions. Our mission is to develop the potential of new generations, and our aim is to improve education through sports, art, communication, technology, culture and civic projects. To date, through a wide and diversified range of programmes, we are giving help to around 400,000 children and adolescents in all regions of the country.

However, when we consider the huge and complex problems our country is facing at the beginning of a new and disturbing century and millennium, the Ayrton Senna Institute can do very little. Our main goal is to fight for a development model able to reconcile productive transformation with social equity. To achieve this goal, we are making a continuous effort to instil in the human consciousness, in the social sensibility, an ethic of co-responsibility between the three pillars of social life: the government, the business world and the non-profit social organisations.

Our vision is to make available to our entire population, but particularly to the young, the fruits, the achievements, of liberal democracy. Only in this way can we bring together the diverse people of our country and reconcile the whole population with all that is great about the richness of our identity. Only in this way can we then contribute to a future world of increased tolerance, justice and peace among nations.

258   **Viviane Senna**
Psychologist. President of the Ayrton Senna Foundation.

Born in 1958 in Brasil. Graduated in Psychology at Pontifícia Universidade Católica in São Paulo. Member of the board of directors of numerous Brazilian charities.

JAN PHILIPP REEMTSMA

TOLERANCE:
WHERE SOMETHING IS MISSING

> Tolerating people with other beliefs
> should not be seen as something admirable,
> but as something completely ordinary.
> *Campe*

The *word* tolerance has a good ring to it, especially if you do not have to think too much about what it means. If "tolerance" signified no more than an attitude of indifference, an attitude of "live-and-let-die", it would hardly be worth mentioning. There are two prerequisites for having "tolerance" in a political sense: one party must be doing the tolerating and one must be tolerated. In most cases, these two parties are not equally powerful. The more powerful party is tolerant under two conditions: it disagrees with the beliefs and actions of the party being tolerated; it would be able to persecute or terrorise the tolerated party in order to subjugate or "convince" it, but chooses of its own will not to do so.[1] Behaviour *cannot* be considered tolerant when a majority is either *forced* by law to cooperate with a despised minority or when it has no opportunity or reason to let its distaste turn into acts of terror or harassment. Similarly, behaviour cannot be considered tolerant when the more powerful party is convinced it could profit by learning from the less powerful religion or culture. Behaviour, however, may be considered tolerant in the broadest sense of the word when two or more equally powerful factions that have the potential to inflict considerable and lasting damage to each other nevertheless choose not to do so.

The concept of tolerance came into being when people began to value peace in their country more than the conformity of their religious beliefs, although moral and religious freedoms were still not protected by law. At that time, to ask for tolerance meant to request that a sovereign *allow* something he was not willing to *guarantee*.

The modern idea of tolerance dates back to the 16th century, specifically to Martin Luther. It was he who adopted the Latin word "tolerantia" as "tollerantz" in German and made it possible to turn it into a political goal. At the same time, Luther proved to be an eloquent opponent of such a new goal: "Gospel is a heavenly treasure that will not tolerate another treasure beside itself" or "Charitas omnia suffert, omnia tolerat, fides nihil suffert et verbum nihil tolerat" (Love endures everything and tolerates everything, faith puts up with nothing, and the word tolerates no divergence).[2] Luther drew a line between *concordia fidei,* or "a unity of faith," and *concordia caritatis,* which we might call "a communal unity" and which, while desirable politically, still conflicted with Luther's contemporary moral norms and the perception of true faith. Yet, by differentiating between these two concepts, he fostered the idea of tolerance despite his continued emphasis on the importance of intolerance: "In this way – i.e., by splitting the concept of *concordia* – he helped create an important prerequisite for a state of mind that may be called a basic inclination towards tolerance. So tolerance became feasible only when disagreement was legitimised as a political way of life."[3]

The Augsburg Religious Peace Treaty of 1555 first formulated the principle of *cuius regio eius religio* – i.e., the religion of the sovereign determines that of his subjects. This principle represented the first step towards what was to become reality only at the end of the Thirty Years' War in Central Europe: the rule of politics over religion. At the same time, the principle made it possible to exert political pressure to achieve religious aims. In order to create a balance, a *ius emigrationis* was agreed upon, the right to emigrate in order to settle in a region dominated by a different religion. The inherent conflict between the right of the sovereign to force his subjects to accept his own religion and the right of his subjects to escape this by emigrating made it urgently necessary to put the principle of tolerance into practice: "The idea of making tolerance into a duty of the state arose not from the concept of tolerance itself but from the rivalry of both major confessions."[4]

By confirming the Augsburg Peace Treaty, the Westphalia Peace Treaty of 1648 reinforced the restrictions imposed on the individual's choice of religion; at the same time, it made a distinction between the obligation to conform to the sovereign's religion and freedom of choice in the private practice of faith. The latter was to be tolerated, albeit as an exception, as indicated by a newly-coined expression "freedom of conscience".[5]

This exception was hailed as a royal virtue by numerous authors, one of whom, Friedrich Wilhelm von Brandenburg, said as early as 1645: "We are sensible enough, God be praised, not to deem ourselves lords of the conscience of our subjects, but instead to leave this to God alone". Or as Christian Thomasius said in 1696: "The duty of a sovereign includes upholding the peace in his state. It does not necessitate bringing and leading those subjects who are convinced of the wrong Christian religion to the truly beatific one."[6]

We can learn a lot by following the evolution of Prussian laws on religion, originally known as Woellner's Religious Edict of July 1788, which defined Prussia's political stance on religious matters. In his edict, Woellner pointed out the differences between "the three major confessions of Christianity" on the one hand, and "other sects and religious factions" on the other. While the former – Catholics, Lutherans and Calvinists – enjoyed particular protection from the monarchy, the latter – Jews, "Herrenhuters", Mennonites and the Bohemian Brethren – were to be treated in accordance with the "tolerance that has always been an integral attribute of Prussian states", and which embodied the principle that "no

262 force was to be applied to their conscience, as long as every one of them peacefully fulfilled his duties as a good citizen of the state, while keeping his particular beliefs to himself and taking great care not to spread the same or to persuade others to become unsettled or shaken in their own faith."[7] Thus, the major Christian confessions were allowed to practice and propagate their religion in public, with the state guaranteeing not only their right to exist, but also their preservation; meanwhile, the religious minorities were allowed to practice their religion, but not to propagate it or even display it in public. The Common Laws of the Prussian States, adopted in June of 1794, continued to distinguish between church organisations ("Kirchengesellschaften") that were treated as "privileged corporations" and those viewed as "private associations". The latter were not simply tolerated, but – just like registered associations – were entered into official books after a due application process had been completed and certain formalities had been observed.[8] In this way tolerance, which Woellner's Religious Edict described as "respect for an observed tradition, nevertheless kept within the sovereign's purview", assumed the dimension of a legal process.

Once civil rights gained in importance, the sovereign's privilege of exercising tolerance became questionable. As the Marquis de Mirabeau declared on August 22, 1789 (and it is hardly possible to express it better today): "I do not want to preach tolerance here. The completely unrestricted freedom of religion is such a holy right in my eyes that the word 'tolerance' which we use to describe it strikes me as tyrannical. For the mere existence of some power that can grant tolerance diminishes freedom of thought, because it has the power not only to grant, but also to refuse tolerance."[9] At the time, tolerance meant dealing with a social deficit in a moral and disinterested manner. As long as such deficits were the rule rather than the exception, the best one could do was to manage the situation disinterestedly and thereby earn praise. But wherever the rule of law became assured – as it did in other countries – tolerance ceased to be a virtue, and praising it meant little more than simply extolling the flaws of the constitutional state.

There is another interpretation of the concept of tolerance which defines it as a specific attitude towards fellow human beings or "tolerance from the heart" (as Eulogius Schneider called it). Such an interpretation is based on a dislike of the cold formality of bureaucratic language typical of the legalese that protects the equality of different confessions or cultural identities. This kind of tolerance seeks a warmer approach towards fellow human beings.[10] However, although the same word "tolerance" is used, it now contains the notion of an assertive interest in diversity driven by the desire to learn from strangers and possibly even to assimilate their novel qualities into one's own value system. But if your "tolerance from the heart" does not focus on the latter, then it is somewhat voyeuristic and insulting, since all you are doing is watching exotic strangers and perhaps seeking a vicarious thrill.

Such "tolerance from the heart" might be recommendable, but it is hardly enforceable, least of all legally. Its underlying premise – dissatisfaction over a legally substandard state of affairs – is based on a specific problem: "Since written laws demand *law-abiding* behaviour, they have to be *legitimate*. Although laws usually fail to say why citizens should actually obey them, such obedience should become possible at any time simply out of respect for the law."[11] So any legal measure that aims to eradicate a deficit of tolerance will function well only if it is accepted as an integral element of a widely shared component of common culture. This assumes quite a lot, including the presence of a positive attitude in the society towards legislative processes that adopt such legal measures.

Yet nothing can reduce the positive value of limitations that are imposed on the propagation of *one's own* beliefs or way of life. "In a complex society, one culture can compete with others only by convincing its own younger generations, who are free to reject its arguments, that its mind is open to the

264

world and that its strength comes from action. There can and should be no protection of cultural species."[12] This is true for the culture of majority as well as for minority social groups. But it can function successfully only as long as a group with a specific cultural identity tries to survive by keeping this identity attractive to its members and by giving it a chance to attract others. A central element of such a cultural identity has to go beyond a simple refusal to exert pressure and must call for the total rejection of anything that could possibly be considered manipulation. Phrased as an imperative it would be: thou shalt not act "intolerantly" because such behaviour will harm your own beliefs and cultural preferences. Based on this attitude, classrooms should be kept free of all religious missionising attempts. And if a teacher wears a headscarf, we should consider this a fashion issue as we do in the case of people who wear a cross on a necklace. None of this should be of any concern to school authorities.

Finally, the idea that rather than tolerating each other, confessions and ways of life should vie with each other to be more attractive to outsiders is central to the so-called "Parable of the Ring" in Lessing's *Nathan the Wise*:

> *Vor grauen Jahren lebt ein Mann in Osten,*
> *Der einen Ring von unschätzbarem Werth*
> *Aus lieber Hand besaß. Der Stein war ein*
> *Opal, der hundert schöne Farben spielte,*
> *Und hatte die geheime Kraft, vor Gott*
> *Und Menschen angenehm zu machen, wer*
> *In dieser Zuversicht ihn trug...*[13]

Those who lack such confidence need to practice mutual tolerance if they do not want to destroy the legal environment designed to remove the inconveniences of tolerance.

Whenever someone starts talking about the virtue of tolerance, be aware: this means something is missing.

1 See also: John Horton (art.), "Toleration", in: Edward Craig (General Editor), *Routledge Encyclopedia of Philosophy*, London/New York 1998, vol. 9, pp. 429; and Dieter Teichert (art.), "Toleranz", in: Jürgen Mittelstraß (Ed.) *Enzyklopädie Philosophie und Wissenschaftstheorie*, Stuttgart/Weimar 1996, vol. 4, pp. 316.

2 Quoted from: "Toleranz": Otto Brunner, Werner Conze, Reinhart Kosellek (Eds.), *Geschichtliche Grundbegriffe. Historisches Lexikon zur politisch-sozialen Sprache in Deutschland*, vol. 6, Stuttgart 1990, pp. 477.

3 Winfried Schulze, "Pluralisierung als Bedrohung: Toleranz als Lösung", in: Heinz Duchhardt (Ed.), *Der Westfälische Friede*, Munich 1998, p. 125.

4 Ibid., p. 127.

5 *Geschichtliche Grundbegriffe*, p. 496.

6 Ibid., pp. 496.

7 Ibid., p. 508.

8 Ibid., p. 509.

9 Ibid., p. 553.

10 Ibid.

11 Jürgen Habermas, "Anerkennungskämpfe im modernen Rechtstaat", in: Charles Taylor, *Multikulturalismus und die Politik der Anerkennung*, Frankfurt/Main, 1997, p. 163.

12 Jürgen Habermas, "Begründete Enthaltsamkeit. Gibt es postmetaphysische Antworten auf die Frage nach dem 'richtigen Leben'?", in: Jürgen Habermas. *Die Zukunft der menschlichen Natur. Auf dem Weg zu einer liberalen Eugenik?*, Frankfurt/Main 2001, p. 13.

13 Gotthold Efraim Lessing, *Nathan der Weise. Ein dramatisches Gedicht in fünf Aufzügen*, Berlin 1779, pp. 120.
Ages ago, a man lived in the east,/ who owned a ring, immensely valuable,/ a gift of his beloved. Its stone was/ an opal, which played in a hundred shades of beauty,/ and had the secret power/ to make him loved by God and men/ whoever wore it with confidence...

Jan Philipp Reemtsma
Philosopher. President of the Hamburg Institute for Social Research. Professor of New German Literature at the University of Hamburg. Winner of the Lessing Prize of the City of Hamburg (1997).

266   Born in 1952 in Bonn, Germany. Specialised in German studies and philosophy at the Hamburg University. Founded and
headed the Arno Schmidt Foundation since 1981.

Selected publications: *In the Cellar* (1999); *Die Auschwitz-
Hefte* (1987, revised in 1994); *Folter. Zur Analyse eines
Herrschaftsmittels* (ed., 1991); *Mord am Strand. Allianzen
von Zivilisation und Barbarei* (1998); *Wie hätte ich mich ver-
halten? und andere nicht nur deutsche Fragen* (2001).

Two things are boundless:
the universe and man's stupidity.
Although I'm still not sure
about the universe.

ALBERT EINSTEIN

Markus Lüpertz (*1941), From the Small Street – dithyrambic, 1967

EPILOGUE

MUHAMMAD ALI

A MESSAGE OF PEACE

Worldwide peace has been my lifelong passion. True peace is more than an absence of war. It comes from an honest appreciation and love for everyone, no matter what their race, religion or politics. It is only when we open ourselves to the possibility of love for everyone we encounter – family, friends and strangers – that we can expect true and lasting peace.

My whole adult life has been dedicated to peace – from the 1960s when I faced prison and the loss of my title because I believed the war in Vietnam was wrong, up to this morning when I prayed that all the people of the world could learn to love one another.

When I meet a new person, I don't see a race or religion – I look deeper. Souls tell the truth about a person. Look into people's eyes, and you will see into their souls. Once you begin to make that essential connection to other people, you will find it impossible to contemplate waging war against them.

Far too many people of the world live in fear that they won't live to see tomorrow. We must learn to satisfy our conflicts peacefully and to respect one another. I continue to work towards these goals daily, and will be able to focus even more intensely on them when the Muhammad Ali Center

274 opens in my hometown of Louisville, Kentucky. Through the Ali Center and the Muhammad Ali Institute of Conflict Resolution and Peacemaking at the University of Louisville, peace will be taught and championed for everyone from children to world leaders. It is a big goal, but it is worth fighting for. As we enter the new millennium, I truly believe the greatest is yet to come...

Muhammad Ali

Boxer. Winner of "Lifetime Achievement Award" of Amnesty International. Named "UN Messenger of Peace" by the United Nations. Voted "Sportsman of the Century" by the BBC.

Born in 1942 as Cassius Clay in Louisville, KY. Won the gold medal in medium-weight boxing at the 1960 Olympic Games. Became the world champion in heavyweight boxing in 1964. Changed his name to Muhammad Ali and converted to Islam in the same year. Refused military draft in 1967. Arrested, stripped of his sports titles and disqualified. Returned to boxing in 1970. Won historic match against George Foreman in 1974 and another against Joe Frazier in 1975. Left active sports in 1981.

APPENDIX

What is the truth?
asked Pilatus – but he didn't wait
around for the answer.

FRANCIS BACON

Rainer Fetting (*1949), Girl und Vogel, 1982